Discovering BTS
An unexpected journey

Discovering BTS
an unexpected journey

방 탄 소 년 단 발 견

예 기 치 않 은 여 정

Marion J Chard

Cover Illustration
Marion J Chard

Proud Daughter Publishing   Alger, MI

Copyright © 2022 by Marion J Chard

All rights reserved. No part of this publication may be reproduced, distributed, or transmitted in any form or by any means, including photocopying, recording, or other electronic or mechanical methods, without the prior written permission of the publisher, except in the case of brief quotations embodied in critical reviews and certain other noncommercial uses permitted by copyright law. For permission requests, please write to the publisher.

Marion J Chard
Proud Daughter Publishing
1460 Joy St
Alger, MI 48610

prouddaughterllc.com

Publisher's Note: Although this publication is designed to provide accurate information in regard to the subject matter covered, the publisher and the author assume no responsibility for errors, inaccuracies, omissions, or any other inconsistencies herein. The content within these pages merely reflects the views/opinions of the author and individuals who shared their stories, and by no means is representative of BTS or HYBE.

Book/cover design & illustration © Marion J Chard
Copyrighted images/illustrations © depositphotos
Chapter photos @Marion J Chard & Kai-Ann Carney
Other images courtesy @ARMY

ISBN 978-0-578-33256-7 Printed in the U.S.A
Library of Congress Control Number: 2021925137

Dedicated to IBIS
My favorite Twitter DM'ers

Lynn, Marsha, Pauline
Vickie, & Wendie

&

Gail never got to see her story in print. Covid took the lives of both she and her husband in Dec 2021, leaving behind a son, Ryan, and daughter, Sara. ARMY will never forget your kind and loving spirit. Borahae, my friend.

In Loving Memory
@GailBTS9

Acknowledgments

The acknowledgments for this book are longer than my arm, therefore for a complete list; please visit my website at: discoveringbts.com.

Kudos to:

Jessica and Kai-Ann Carney for instigating my love affair with BTS. It all began with you. There would be no one else to thank if not for that first glimpse into Bangtan heaven.

My husband Lee for tolerating my obsessiveness, and eventually succumbing to the fact that you'd have to live with it. You've been wonderful!

My numerous Twitter followers who helped me share information about my project, and those with whom I formed lasting friendships along the way.

All who contributed their stories for the website and the book.

@Somin_Park007 for translating the book title to Hangul
방탄소년단 발견   예기치 않은 여정

Susan Finn @HappyOlderArmy for being my second, all important set of eyes, and good friend. Thank you for your time, effort, and editing skills.

Donna @btsmommy305 for her wonderful idea of adding whales to the sky in the cover image. That was the icing on the cake.

My web sponsor The Comfy Sweatshirt. Thank you for backing me. I hope our joint venture is profitable for both of us. Please check out Bess' online ETSY store. She's not only creative but a sweet person too and was kind enough to donate a couple BTS designs for my giveaways!

My special DM—IBIS (acronym for Itty-Bitty Inspiration Squad)—without our group of six, this book would never have come to fruition. First is Lynn @Whisper1204. You were the one who initially inspired me "You should write a book!", and for that, I am forever grateful. And of course, the other four beautiful human beings, Pauline @popfrench_7, Wendie @goldilocks81, Marsha @angylize and Vickie @Vickie7BTS, who continually lift me up each day. What would life be without you? Admit it, I just made you cry.

Affinity Publisher - because this entire book including the cover were created using their wonderful software.

And last, but certainly not least (they always say to save the best for last!) BTS members, Kim Nam-joon, Kim Seok-jin, Min Yoon-gi, Jung Ho-seok, Park Ji-min, Kim Tae-hyung, & Jeon Jung-kook. After all, you are the spark that lit the fire, and the subject of this book. My eternal thanks and love saturate these pages.

Preface

In March 2021, I created a website, discoveringbts.com. My goal was to collect stories from ARMY regarding how they discovered BTS, and eventually to include many of those along with mine.

So, what's up with the title? It simply means that while we may start down any path in life, our journey rarely follows a straight line. We often stumble upon roads with numerous unopened doors and unexpected adventures. Discovering BTS has been no exception to this rule, because not only did it turn me onto their music, but they continue to enrich my daily life with their philosophical and infectious positive outlook, keen sense of humor, generosity of heart, and their down-to-earth attitudes. Through them I've met many wonderful people, and in turn established numerous long-lasting friendships. Finally, BTS motivated me to write this book and subsequently to reach out to you for your inspiring stories.

Warning: Reading this book could lead you down that slippery slope into the world of Bangtan. It happened to me. It could happen to you. Don't say you weren't forewarned.

Borahae!

P.S. Remember the website will remain active, so you still have a chance to share your story with BTS and me.

Contents

Down the Rabbit Hole	1
Happy Mother's Day	3
Bingeing	17
Covid Rears Its Head	21
Their Stories (refer to index for indiv story pgs)	40
Information	232
An Afterword	243

Down the Rabbit Hole

I began the fall down the proverbial rabbit hole on a visit to see family in Atlanta, Georgia in October of 2018. "Hey Nana, you want to watch some videos of my favorite group?" Little did I know how that fateful question would open a door that would affect the rest of my life.

I was familiar with the name, only because my stepdaughter and granddaughter attended a BTS concert at Citifield a few weeks earlier; however, that was the extent of my knowledge. I wondered at the time why they would travel all the way to New York, just to see a boy band. What was their overpowering appeal? I would soon learn the strength of that allure.

At first, there was some hesitation. I was curious of course, but I mostly did it to be kind ("ya, sure hun"), however, I must divulge they were damned cute. So, the three of us sat in my stepdaughter's home office and watched one video, which became two, and then before I knew it, an hour or more had passed. Hey, I stated, I like *that* song.

Well, two days later, I was asking (shh, begging) to watch yet another. Soon we were behind closed doors once more, staring, drooling, and making flirtatious remarks about these handsome young men. I was beginning to comprehend their indisputable and infectious adoration of BTS. But wait, it wasn't just their looks (though that certainly didn't hurt), but they could actually sing and dance. I was impressed with their raw talent and their professionalism—the music was new and refreshing. Then my son-in-law entered the room and saw the look on my face. "Oh gawd, it's a contagion", he sighed aloud, and left shaking his head. Evidently, he was all too familiar with those blank stares and dreamy expressions. Yes, it was all over and although he knew it, I had no idea what was in store for me. However, I gave in and disclosed I was a tad smitten.

Over the next few days, they challenged me to learn their names. "Oh, don't worry Nana, you'll get it." "Impossible", I replied, because just when I thought I was able to name one or two, they'd change their hair and/or their eye color. However, Jimin stood out among the rest. He caught my eye as he gyrated across the screen. "What's his name?" Okay, one down, six to go, and like that, I had a bias. Yes, just one of the terms I would learn over my course of *study*.

While it was difficult getting to know who was who (as with any other group), I had the most trouble differentiating between Jungkook and V. To me they looked like brothers, especially with their natural brown hair color. Then there was J-Hope. After, Jimin, he was the easiest to pick out of the bunch because of those beautiful, prominent cheekbones, but it only worked when he was smiling. This wasn't going to be an easy task. Then they threw a monkey wrench at me—these were only their stage names. C'mon, I was just getting the hang of this! I had some homework to do. But before I left their house, they sent me home with a poster, which still hangs in my she shed. Call it premeditated indoctrination. I'm onto you girls. I know what you're up to.

Happy Mother's Day

If someone would have told me back then that I'd be writing a book about this group three years later, I would have fallen on the floor laughing. Not that I thought they were a joke. Far from it. I liked them. However, I would have never guessed what an impact they would have on me. C'mon, they were just another group I might listen to now and then, or so I thought…

You see, I'm a writer, and had already published several historical-related articles, and most recently The Story of Q, a tween sci-fi series involving a ten-year old girl and her accidental discovery of a portal into another world. I also edited several books for other authors, including a philosophy book on Jesus and Socrates. Yes, a far cry from the book you're currently reading. Ah, variety is the spice of life.

I must admit, that after I returned home, I felt self-conscious sitting in front of my computer, performing searches for BTS on YouTube. I would have felt embarrassed if my friends caught me doing so. I'd imagine what they'd say. "Gawd Marion, what the hell are you watching?" or "Gee, aren't they a little young for you?" or "Uh, when did you start liking boy bands?" Blush! But that didn't stop me from sneaking peeks when I was alone in my office. The more I watched, the more I wanted to see and hear. The only ones I could confide in were my stepdaughter and Jessica. It was my insidious little secret.

As the weeks passed and winter became spring, I created my first BTS playlist, but it remained private—certainly not displayed within my public directory of various music videos, history, tech, science, and gardening interests on YouTube. Again, how could I explain my attraction?

Discovering BTS

Some of the first songs I added were: War of Hormone, Mic Drop, Boy in Luv, Boy with Luv, Blood, Sweat and Tears, Fake Love, DNA, Spring Day, Fire, We Are Bulletproof Part 2, and Idol. Part of WAB Part 2 became our thing. One of us would text, "click click", and the other would respond, "bang bang".

I began to realize the scope of their talent. Not just their precise and exquisite dance moves, but I was impressed with the variety of their songs. Compare the comforting and beautiful melody of Spring Day to Mic Drop's heavy rap and thunder! They were no fluke, and I liked both sides of them—the yin and yang. That surprised me too because I was never a big fan of rap. There were some I liked, but they were few and far between, even though I love a broad spectrum of music from classical - Bach, Beethoven, and Mozart to rock - Beatles, Fleetwood Mac, and Tom Petty, to alternative/grunge - Nirvana, Pearl Jam, and Stone Temple Pilots, to folk/bluegrass - Allison Krause, Mary Chapin Carpenter, and The Wailin' Jennys, and everything in between including Ed Sheeran, John Mayer, and Nickel Creek... well, you get the drift. I have eclectic taste.

I had no idea what the lyrics were (except for the English text of course), but I knew that I liked what I heard. Eventually, I discovered there were videos posted on YouTube with English translations. They were helpful, and it gave more meaning to the songs. Ah, another step closer.

I was clueless regarding the extent of their popularity. Would this be another band that came and went with the wind? I didn't know their fandom had a special name, nor was I aware that soon I'd be extending my vocabulary with new words or additional meanings such as wrecker, ARMY, Festa, fan chant, maknae, hyung and muster. Soon another door would open into the fascinating world of BTS. I had only just begun to get a glimpse into their expanding universe.

"Do you want to go to Chicago?"

"Sure", I responded. "That sounds like fun. What's going on?"

"We're planning a trip in May, and…"

It would be a trip for the whole family, but there was more to it. "Uh, we got you a ticket to see BTS, for Mother's Day!"

Whoa!

Well, this was out of the blue and most certainly unexpected. I was going to a BTS concert. Okay. I was excited but had a lot of mixed feelings. I wanted to see them perform, but in my head I could picture tens of thousands of young kids and me. Would I feel out of place with everyone looking at me saying, "What in the world is she doing here?" Gulp!

For one thing, I swore I would never attend another super concert at a stadium. I'd had my fill of them over the years. Usually the sound was awful, and all you could see were tiny figures on a tiny stage. Look, there they are. Can you pass me the binoculars? I was in love with the smaller venues like Detroit's Fox Theater or Masonic Temple.

Over the next few months, I tried to learn as much as I could. I listened to every video I could find, and my granddaughter would quiz me at regular intervals—I was finally able to name each of them. And much to my surprise, I began picking out their individual singing voices. But I was still in my infancy, I was baby ARMY, though I didn't know the term yet. I never knew liking a band had such a steep learning curve!

Discovering BTS

There we were in Chicago, with the day of the concert fast approaching and I still felt apprehensive. I couldn't stop thinking about not fitting in. Even in my band days (guitar/bass and vocals), there were still times that I felt self-conscious walking into a room, and now I would be entering an entire stadium of only tweens and teens (or so I thought). I wanted to go, but I guess I would have to pull up my big girl pants and tough it out, right?

Then Kai-Ann and Jessica starting talking about merch. "We have to go to the stadium today and go early because there will be thousands of people in line..." Oh joy. For mid-May, the weather wasn't being very cooperative for one thing, and the thought of standing in line for hours didn't thrill me either, but I was game.

We went and it was fun. The sight of so many happy, excited people, many adorned in BTS buttons, hats, and shirts, was a something to see. I began feeling a bit more comfortable. Their fans were dedicated, and their enthusiasm was contagious. It's hard to explain unless you experience it for yourself. And of course, Jessica was in heaven. You could hear it in her voice and see it in her eyes.

The night of the concert, we were all excited, but I was still leery because the Weather Channel predicted temperatures in the mid-thirties. It didn't look promising. Now I was not only nervous, but I wasn't looking forward to sitting in Soldier Field (an outdoor facility) in winter-like weather. I think our husbands thought we were nuts, but we bundled up, called an Uber and off we went.

There was some initial confusion when we first arrived. Evidently the people running the event weren't sure what door our section ticket holders were supposed to use, and we were sent back and forth a few times until they finally let us in. Cheers all around. However, it wasn't an unpleasant experience because we got to meet other ARMY, and everyone was eager to help and so friendly. We were in this together.

"These seats are great! How did you manage this?" I was sitting in sec 205, row 3, seat 11. I wasn't expecting to be sitting this close. Everyone around us was bundled up for the weather. They held precious BTS tickets, and nothing was going to deter their fun or enthusiasm. It was off to a good start, despite the plummeting temperatures.

Then the big screens lit up the night and music videos filled the stadium. They looked so beautiful and larger than life. They weren't even on stage, yet the crowd was already roaring. I could see that this wasn't going to be an ordinary performance. Nothing prepared me for what was going to happen next.

"I know I'm going to cry", Jessica blurted as soon as she caught sight of the stage for Dionysus. The performance was impeccable down to every detail. If I closed my eyes it was as though I was listening to my headphones at home. Every note was sheer perfection. Everyone can sound great in a studio. You can do as many takes as needed and everything can be tweaked via a mixing board. But when you're able to bring that sound to a live performance, well, that's sheer talent and it's rare. And to do it while dancing, that's another level of excellence bar none. I often want to ask, "How long was it before you could easily sing while dancing at the same time?" ARMY, try it at home without getting out of breath—it's not easy.

The concert made an indelible impression on me. The lights, the music, the sound system, the dancing, the videos, the camerawork, the crowd—everything about it.

And then there were the fan chants.

"Kim Namjoon! Kim Seokjin! Min Yoongi! Jung Hoseok! Park Jimin! Kim Taehyung! Jeon Jungkook! BTS!" and repeat "Kim Namjoon! Kim Seokjin! Min Yoongi! Jung Hoseok! Park Jimin! Kim Taehyung! Jeon Jungkook! BTS!"

Discovering BTS

And during Fake Love...

"I'm so sorry but it's Fake Love" "FAKE LOVE"

"Fake Love" "FAKE LOVE" "Fake Love"

Everything was so organized! And they had a REAL band backing them up. I didn't know it at the time, but this was Ghost. You never saw them, but you heard them. Make no mistake about that. Live music, no lip-syncing. This was stage production at its finest. Much later I learned that approximately 250 people are behind the scenes making this all possible, from ideas, to implementation, which included enormous, majestic cats during Dionysus, a giant bubble that Jimin sat inside during the beginning of Serendipity, huge slides that the guys played upon, and even Jungkook flying over the crowd during Euphoria. Everything was breathtaking.

However, no matter how fascinating, mother nature held no pity. Even BTS joked as they spoke to us, "Welcome to the winter tour", they laughed while trying to keep warm in between songs. We often held hands and stamped our feet to retain the heat. I'd lie if I said that our rosy glows were strictly because of BTS, however, the near freezing temps played a large role too. And we even made our own fan chant, "Oh my, my, my, can't feel my thigh!" That's one we'll never forget.

While every song worked its way into my soul, the vocal line's solos stood out among the rest, like Jin singing and playing piano during Epiphany. I never realized he could play. Then V's mesmerizing performance of Singularity. The choreography along with his sultry voice was enough to knock anyone over. And of course, Jimin popping himself out of his bubble during Serendipity and hitting the sweetest of notes, and finally Jungkook flying over the awed crowd while his tender, but strong voice rang throughout Euphoria.

Every portion of the show was spectacular, but Boy With Luv will always hold a special place in my heart. The melody speaks to me, and I find the song's construction/composition, fascinating. Most modern songs follow a very simple formula (or similar), which usually goes, verse, chorus, verse, chorus, bridge, and chorus. But Boy with Luv (as well as other BTS songs), break away from this mold. BWL begins with an intro, then flows into verse, verse, pre-chorus, chorus, post-chorus, verse, verse, pre-chorus, chorus, post-chorus, bridge, chorus, and finally post-chorus. Next time you listen to it, see if you can hear all the changes within the song. But I'll talk more about this later in the book.

Of course, I must mention Suga's famous one-liner in Fire—Bultaoreune!!! When I hear that it sends shivers down my spine. How about you? Bow, wow, wow!

Another thing that surprised me was how talkative BTS was with their fans. Several times during the night, they'd stop, walk the length of the stage, and back, and simply engage with ARMY! Sometimes they'd even talk to us in English. Ah, not that it mattered to me. Korean or English, I just loved hearing their sweet voices. They loved being there, and they adored their fans as much as their fans adored them. This was yet another thing that enamored my heart.

I could discuss the concert for hours; however, I'll end this chapter by saying that the finale's combined performance of Make it Right and Mikrokosmos was the perfect way to say goodbye. And to this day, whenever I hear those two songs, I'm quickly transported back to that unforgettable evening, all over again. If you've ever "been in the zone", you'll understand my meaning. I think I literally floated out the concert doors (or at least it felt that way), never to be the same again.

I was a Girl with Luv!

Love Yourself: Speak Yourself Setlist
Soldier Field, Chicago, IL.

Act 1

Video Introduction: Dionysus
1. Dionysus
2. Not Today
3. Outro: Wings (extended)

Act II

Video interlude: J-Hope & Jungkook focus
4. Trivia: Just Dance - performed by J-Hope
5. Euphoria - performed by Jungkook
6. Best of Me

Act III

Video Interlude: Jimin & RM focus
7. Serendipity - performed by Jimin
8. Trivia: Love - performed by RM
9. Boy With Luv
10. Dope (shortened)
11. Silver Spoon (shortened)

12. Fire (shortened)
13. IDOL (remix)

Act IV

Video Interlude: V focus
14. Singularity – performed by V
15. Fake Love

Act V

Video Interlude: Suga and Jin focus
16. Trivia: Seesaw – performed by Suga
17. Epiphany – performed by Jin
18. The Truth Untold – performed by Jin, Jimin, V & Jungkook
19. Outro: Tear – performed by Suga, J-Hope, & RM
20. MIC Drop (remix with extended outro)

Encore:

Video Interlude: Group focus
21. Anpanman
22. So What
23. Make it Right
24. Mikrokosmos (with extended outro)

SF0511
$93CCTX
$ 21.50
SECTION/AISLE
205
ZWS185X
ROW SEAT
3 11
7331015
B 4MAR9
SECTION/AISLE ROW/BOX SEAT ADMISSION EVENT CODE
205 3 11 B 180.00 ESF0511
VI
GATE 38 CLUB
CN 59383
LIVE NATION PRESENTS
BTS WORLD TOUR
'LOVE YOURSELF:
SPEAK YOURSELF'
SOLDIER FIELD-CHICAGO, IL
SAT MAY 11 2019 7:30PM
205
BEARS1
3
180.00
11
19727570389O
BUY TICKETS AT TICKETMASTER.COM
ticketmaster

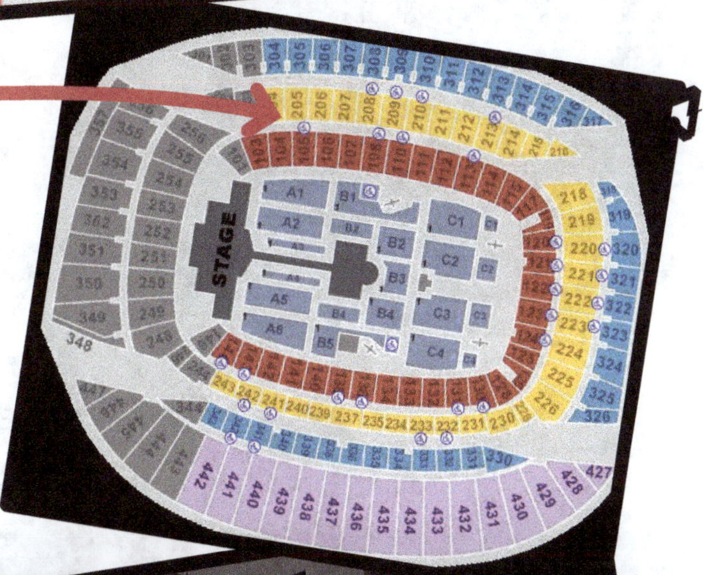
STAGE

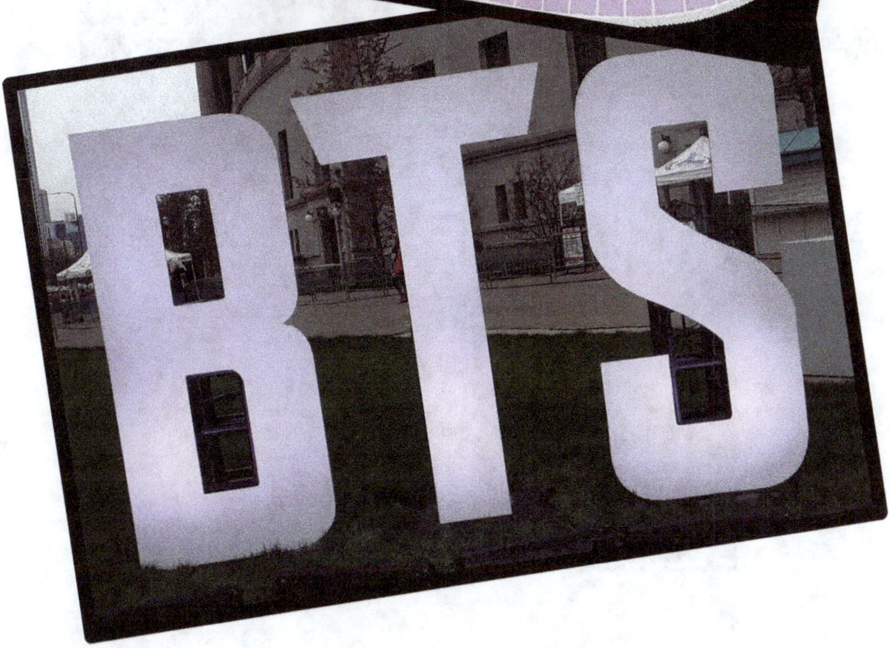
BTS

Jessica's new BTS shoestrings

Yours Truly

Bingeing

Attending the concert in May 2019 further fueled my fire and I found myself watching even more videos on YouTube. But I was still a lone sheep, and not connected to BTS or ARMY except through my Georgia family. They were the only ones to whom I could talk. However, 2019 would open my eyes on another level and introduce me to others who shared my passion.

In June, my granddaughter invited me to stay with her for a few days while her parents celebrated their anniversary in another state. Of course, the first thing on our list (well it was the only thing on our list), was BTS. In other words, a BTS extravaganza. Other than taking a few breaks to eat and sleep (those pesky requirements), it was nothing but BTS for the next forty-eight hours, plus. We watched DVDs and music videos and I even learned the choreo for the chorus for Boy With Luv. I made a promise to do this, and I kept it, even though I felt a bit silly doing so, but I had so much fun. I could be crazy and be me. We laughed a lot and really bonded during my stay. And when her parents returned, Jessica and I performed BWT for Kai-Ann. I felt like a kid again. Oh my, my, my!

And during one of my visits, I was introduced to the two local K-POP stores in Atlanta. "There's K-POP stores?" That was news to me. Walking in, I was overwhelmed. Everywhere I looked, I saw BTS! There were aisles and aisles of DVDS, CDs, photocards, plushies, posters, keychains, clothing, blankets, sticky notes, and everything you could possibly imagine. Hmmm, let's see, I want one of those, and I must have that, and oh, how adorable is that! Just when I thought I had everything I wanted, Kai-Ann would ask, "Did you see this? You have to get this!" And I did.

While both stores were great, I fell in love with 'KPOP Story' in Suwanee because of the atmosphere. It was smaller and the tiny Korean woman behind the counter had the most infectious personality. She frequently interacted with us, and one time she even danced with us to a BTS song playing on the wall screen. It was also my introduction to Korean ice cream, called Melona (메로나). The honeydew melon ice pops were to die for! We don't have any in our area, but I recently found a recipe on a Korean food site.

"Nana, you have to watch this!" Because she knew of my love for sloths, she had me watch an episode of RUN BTS. It was my introduction to the weekly show. I laughed aloud watching Jimin sprawled on the floor in front of a refrigerator, while the members referred to him as a sloth. And I'll never forget the guys running around yelling, "chicken" at the top of their lungs. And now it's not unusual to hear me shouting "chick-ennnnn", upon entering our family's house during visits to Georgia. Yup, that's little ol' me.

I also discovered that Kai-Ann was learning Korean online. "You're taking Korean lessons?" I found it a bit odd at first, but after a while, I could understand why she was pursuing it. She was also the one who got me to sign up for Twitter. I had an account a couple of years ago, but it wasn't long after that I deleted it. But now because of BTS, I would give it another shot, and that's when my eyes were opened to the world of ARMY!

It was July 2019, when I signed up for an account. At first it was just she and I. Then I noticed her interaction with a few other people she met. I learned all the basics, and eventually reached out to a couple of other members. I was a bit shy in the beginning, but eventually became friends with a few people. I began looking forward to these encounters, because it was finally nice to be able to talk about BTS with others without feeling ashamed or guilty. They were just like me. It was comforting to note that yes, older ARMY did exist. It wasn't all tweens and teens as I initially thought, but people who were doctors, nurses, moms (and dads), and teachers. People from all walks of life who loved BTS as much as I did. I'm proud to say that of the several people I initially met, I'm still friends with to this day.

August 29, 2019. Ah, that was the day I finally admitted (well, er to everyone who followed my blog, Marion's Mumblings), that I loved BTS. It began with the words, "Hmm, where do I start? Oh ya, admitting something to the world. Okay, coming out from the woodwork and conceding that I *love,* BTS! There I said it and no, I'm not ten, fifteen, or even twenty, but I got hooked, all thanks to my stepdaughter and granddaughter..." It was a catharsis. I felt so good and so free that day. It was an unforgettable moment for me. Trust me, I still had a long way to go, but I was off to a good beginning.

While Jessica had her entire room decorated with BTS memorabilia, it was Kai-Ann who gave me the impetus to slowly display a few BTS items in my office like she did. We both share offices with our husbands, so we had to infiltrate with discretion. At first my hubby was like, "Uh, you are really doing this?" Uh-huh, I admitted sheepishly, while enduring his strange looks and eye-rolling. I can do this I said to myself. Just be stealthy. He had his side of the room and I had mine. I was standing my ground.

The first of my last two blog entries of the year was the day after Christmas – 'That Certain Something – J-Hope'. I posted one of my favorite (and still favorite) pictures of him, taken during an outdoor photoshoot. It's the one where he's wrapped snugly in his camel-colored winter coat, with the fur-lined hood framing his beautiful face. I also shared a short video clip and wrote the following words. "Well, anyone who's read my blog, knows that I'm a huge BTS fan, and that J-Hope (Hoseok) is one of my faves. One of his latest photos was posted this week, and must admit, it takes my breath away. I couldn't let it go by the wayside without a mention in my blog. So, here's to moonbeams and daydreams."

The very last entry was 'Happy Birthday Kim Taehyung', a video tribute I created and shared on YouTube, accompanied by Tae's beautiful melody, Winter Bear. And here I sit typing this on his 26th birthday, two years later. How timely.

Luckily I was able to take several trips to Georgia that year, and looking back now, I feel so lucky, as everyone was completely unaware of what lie ahead—disruption, isolation, and tears.

Covid Rears its Head

It's often said that every dark cloud has a silver lining, and this also held true for Covid. While a vast storm brewed, thundering down upon every corner of the earth, still there were good moments that helped carry us through the darkest of times. For me, part of that sun that persisted was the respite I found in BTS.

Yoongi, also touched upon this in 2021, commenting that if it weren't for Covid, he most likely would never have written Daechwita. I understood what he meant. Most of his followers understood his comments, yet some chose to take his words out of context and accused him of being unfeeling while thousands of people suffered and died due to the virus. But his words touched my soul because despite of the situation, he and I could still glean some positivity out of a world spinning out of control. As with any tragedy, you can either let it eat you alive, or take the dragon by the tail and make the best of it. Instead of lamenting his time in isolation, he was inspired to write. I'm positive the song would not have been written if not for COVID. Just as certain novels, songs or paintings would have never been shared with the world if not for sorrowful conditions. Love as well as tragedy bring great things to fruition.

While this chapter seems to have taken a 180 from the previous one, it's simple because life it never simple, black, or white, but filled with thousands of shades of grey. Think of BTS's song, Blue & Grey. There are always dark moments that make us appreciate the lighter ones, and as I write this tonight, a thousand memories flow through my veins. I am reminded that merely four years ago, just prior to me finding BTS, a sudden health scare made me rethink my life and offer thanks for having another chance.

Discovering BTS

To briefly touch on this, my blood pressure shot to 284/224 and I was admitted into cardio ICU after entering the emergency room. Doctors said they couldn't believe that I came out of it without any lasting effects (well except for being on the meds for the rest of my life), yet alone alive. So, each time I look back on this, I am even more grateful to be able to write this book about BTS, and how they made a great life even better. Evidently the universe wasn't ready to recycle my stardust.

While the beginning of 2020 found me blogging about BTS and the inspiration they imparted, March was already wreaking havoc when Covid struck with a vengeance, even assailing my stepdaughter. She was the first person we personally knew infected with this newly discovered virus. Luckily, she recovered, but many weren't as lucky, including an acquaintance who owned a local bar/restaurant. Unfortunately, she lost her life at age 40 due to complications.

I had planned a long-awaited trip with my bestie, Karla. We had scheduled a home and garden tour in Savannah, GA for our April birthdays. Sadly, the trip was canceled, and put on temporary hold. What we didn't know was our vacation would still be on hold at the end of 2021.

While many claimed that their lives were *not* affected by the pandemic, our lives in rural Michigan came to a screeching halt. There were no more visits with friends or family, as we sat sequestrated in our home. Meetings were now held online, and there was little contact with the outside world. Luckily, my husband and I get along famously, and our isolation made us grow even closer.

It was during this time that my focus turned to BTS, as I spent increasing hours online. I had time to carefully listen to each song, catch V-Live and episodes of Run BTS, and expand my friend list on Twitter. I also created short BTS videos and shared them on YouTube. At first they were simply cute birthday tributes, but later in 2021 my edits grew in depth, as BTS continued to inspire me with such songs as Butterfly, Blue and Grey, and Your Eyes Tell.

It was also during this period I learned more about the members within the group. Not only impersonal facts, but got to see them in all their complexity, as true individuals, and I loved what I saw. I think that's a point that's often misunderstood or overlooked by "outsiders" (giggle, giggle, muggles)—the fact that we not only love their music, but we love who they are as people. That's a rare thing, especially when it involves *seven* human beings. It was as though BigHit was not only able to see their talent(s) but also able to discern their true personalities. Talent + personality, a perfectly balanced equation.

Twitter became an outlet for me during this time—I was never lonely because I still felt a connection to the world around me. I became friends with many kindred souls. Eventually, I was able to admit I was older ARMY, and in turn, others did the same. It opened the eyes of many not only on Twitter but through due diligence and patience, *somewhat* altered the media's misconceptions about BTS's fandom.

However, we (older ARMY, anyone over 30) weren't always met with open arms within ARMY's realm. Many were ridiculed and even threatened on the timeline and via direct messaging. Sadly, several older ARMY chose to leave Twitter permanently, while others including myself, took a hiatus, in hope that things would cool down. Unfortunately, as with any kind of social media, it's too easy for people to become one of the nameless millions, hiding behind their keyboards, and lashing out at the world, with little or no fear of consequence. I tried to put it into perspective, and consider the source, nonetheless their words were still hurtful.

While communicating online, a group of us decided that we would do things the old-fashioned way and began sending each other snail-mail. Sometimes we organized card exchanges. Other times, we would send mail to special friends, along with photocards, stickers, and various other goodies. On a few golden occasions, I'd receive an unexpected gift from a sweet soul I hardly knew and would tear up in gratitude. I began asking my hubby, "Did I get any ARMY mail today?" After a few months, he would drop mail off at my desk, exclaiming, "You have ARMY mail". It was and still is a treat.

I entered a few giveaways (GA's) and decided I would hold a few of my own. I offered posters, photocards, and even copies of CD box sets, realizing that some weren't as fortunate as I—they couldn't afford the merch. It was a great feeling to be able to do this and receiving letters of appreciation only added to it. I'm happy I could bring some joy to others.

Even though, I had joined a group chat and talked with others early on, it wasn't until late 2020 when I asked a few specific individuals if they'd like to form a group. We hit it off immediately and soon melded into the Itty-Bitty Inspiration Squad (we're all 5'3" and under). I noticed that its acronym was IBIS, so soon after we adopted the beautiful white bird as our mascot. I even bought an IBIS stuffed animal on EBAY.

Since that fateful day, at least a few of the six, talk to each other daily. And while we don't always agree on everything, we have a deep level of respect for each other, and a love for BTS beyond measure. We not only discuss their music, charm, and abilities, but everything worldly under the sun from A to Z. We've been a source of inspiration, joy, and comfort to each other, and we can't imagine our lives without the other five.

After sending Lynn's (a member of IBIS) daughter a signed copy of the first book of my tween sci-fi series, The Story of Q, she suggested that I should write a book about BTS. While I was flattered, I put the thought aside, but the more I slept on the idea... Hey IBIS, I've given it some serious consideration and maybe, just maybe I *will* do it. Finally in March of 2021, I came up with the idea of discussing how I discovered BTS. In turn I created a website and began asking ARMY to submit their stories. IBIS, true to their name, inspired and encouraged me to carry on. The rest is history, as they say.

After my husband and I redecorated our home office earlier in 2021, I decided that my half would be dedicated to BTS, therefore he built me two sets of shelves to accommodate my collection. One wall holds four clear plastic interchangeable frames, that allow me to swap posters whenever the mood strikes. I also purchased a magnetic board that I fill with items from ARMY. In December it held greetings that I received for Christmas.

One day I received a question from a follower asking if I was the Marion that hung out in the WWII forums. "I saw the name, Proud Daughter Publishing and... could that be you?" Long story short, it was an old friend. We knew each other because of the roles our fathers played during the war, but unfortunately we lost contact years ago. "Can you believe we reunited because of our mutual love of BTS?" I was astounded too. What a coincidence! If it weren't for BTS, we would have never had the opportunity to renew and strengthen our friendship.

Discovering BTS

My love of BTS also sparked my curiosity about all things Korean including food. Whenever I'd visit Atlanta, we'd stop at Kai-Ann and Jessica's favorite Korean restaurant. I already appreciated a variety of cuisine, including Italian, Mexican, mid-eastern and a variety of Asian foods, and it was love at first bite. The first thing I sampled was beef bulgogi, along with numerous side dishes. YUM! Shortly after that I purchased a Korean cookbook, knowing my husband liked trying new dishes too. Two of my favorite meals to cook are beef bulgogi and Korean fried chicken.

Since I spent more time at home due to Covid, I began learning Korean on my own. After trying several methods, I finally found the perfect course of study for me—Learn Korean in Korean with Mr. Kim. I supplemented this with a couple of books I bought on Amazon and later fell in love with Learn Korean with Tiny Tan. I was pleasantly surprised at the simplicity of their alphabet. It was fun sharing the joy of learning with other ARMY on Twitter and asking for advice from those entirely more knowledgeable than me. Again, I'd like to extend my appreciation to @Somin_Park007 for translating the book's title to Hangul.

This also generated interest in the history of the country. While I was familiar with the Korean War in the 1950's (my husband's father was a pilot), reading Korea: The Impossible Country by Daniel Tudor, certainly expanded my horizons. Not only did I learn about the multiple instances of unification and division, their rulers, and invasions from China and Japan, but the book helped me to understand the current Korean mindset. It explained their competitive spirit not only regarding education, but in the workplace. And tying in with my studies, I discovered that Hangul was created by King Sejong during the Joseon Dynasty (1393-1897), who was considered one of the greatest rulers of Korea. He was highly respected for his loving disposition and a passionate scholar and wanted his people to have an easy means of communication, in the hope that it would improve the lives of all his citizens.

In 1446, the first Korean alphabet was proclaimed under the original name Hunmin chong-um, which literally meant "the correct sounds for the instruction of the people." The Korean people never had an appropriate script for their spoken language and until the invention of Hangul, they had used a cumbersome system using Chinese characters for their pronunciation. But Chinese was a language very different from Korean in its vocal patterns and sentence formation and couldn't represent Korean sounds and structure adequately. And mastering the complexity of Chinese characters made the writing system too difficult for those other than the privileged few.

Scouring YouTube one day, I fell upon a song that was unfamiliar to me—"I Like it - Part 2". I was immediately intrigued with the melody and couldn't take my eyes off Hoseok. His moves were so precise. He had a certain je ne sais quoi. I replayed the video many times. How did I overlook this song? It quickly became one of my go-tos, and Hoseok instantly became one of my wreckers. I began fixating on his dancing and was amazed how his body moved with such fluidity.

Another song that escaped my notice until then was Pied Piper. I saw ARMY discussing it on Twitter, and for the first time got to watch a live performance. Again, I was mesmerized by the music and their performance. It was sexy and hypnotic, and I quickly added it to my playlist. How many more treasures were still waiting for me?

It was about the same time that I finally made my private playlist, *public*. I no longer cared if everyone on the internet knew of my love for BTS. They were an important part of my life, just as important as my love for the styles of the 1940's, my interest in science, history, or my joy in tending perennial gardens.

Discovering BTS

Still, I must admit that I was a bit timid whenever someone entered my office, because the first thing they saw was BTS. Of course, they teased me, and I expected it, and took it in stride. However, after repeatedly being teased by the same people, I began to resent it. After a while, a joke is no longer funny and I'm sure many of you understand my wrath. I was tired of hearing people call them girls. I was weary of them asking me why I would bother listening to music I couldn't understand. Their annoying questions were exhausting. Why did I have to keep defending myself? Eventually, I stopped doing so. I knew what I liked, and I loved BTS. Period.

Discovering BTS's solo releases was also a source of great pleasure. I must admit that until this time, I had not paid particular attention to Yoongi. But for some reason, I became very intrigued by all aspects of him. The more I learned about him and the more I listened to his music, etc., well, he became my new bias, and remains so until this day.

The song that immediately caught my attention was So Far Away (the first version I heard was his mix with Jungkook and Jin) with Suran. It's one of my absolute favorites, and I never tire of either version. It's brilliant, and the guitar solo is one of my all-time favorites. There's isn't a note that I'd change and it's the perfect counterpoint to the sweet vocals. Overall, AgustD (released in 2016), was a still a bit heavy for my personal taste, but I still give it a listen.

The transition from his first mix tape to D2 (2020) was phenomenal, and I was astonished by his personal growth. The tracks on AgustD seemed to represent a younger, grittier, and angrier Yoongi, while D2 and others since released (with BTS and collabs), show a mellower and melodic side, while still retaining his edginess. Some I play on a continual rotation are: Eight by IU, (produced by and featuring Suga), Seesaw, People, Suga's Interlude by Halsey, Interlude: Set Me Free, 28, Dear my Friend, and Burn It featuring Max. When I'm in a "heavier" mode, Interlude: Shadow, Daechwita and Give it to Me. Dontcha just love his smirky laugh and sneer?

I also adore listening to him play the piano (think of the Adidas ad and him playing I Need You). That's even my ringtone. Bottom line—if you ever want to get on my good side, just bring over anything related to Yoongi, and I'll be grateful. Bring him in person, and I'll be your buddy for life. 😊

RM's mix tape MONO, is a step beyond. It's one I can listen to it in its entirety. I didn't know what to expect, thinking it would be heavier. This was another side of him I didn't know existed, and it was such a ray of sunshine. Forever Rain is one of my favorites. It sets the tone, grabs you and pulls you in. It makes me feel as though I'm right there, feeling and smelling the rain. I'm listening to it as I type… The guitar riff is simple, yet effective and sweet. Seoul gives us a taste of yin and yang—I love you Seoul/I hate you Seoul. Hasn't everyone experienced mixed feelings? I love the repetition of Everything Goes and how it grows and builds throughout the song until finally falling into quiet slumbers. As he reminds us—nothing lasts forever. It passes… jinaga 지나가

J-Hope's Hello World follows a much different path than his fellow rappers, and like him, it's more upbeat. While some of it is too "poppy" for me, Blue Side (Outro) speaks to me. It's "bluesy" and always leaves me wanting more. My favorite cut is Daydream, filled with sparkling imagery between dreams and wishes for the real world. He talks of fantasy and taking a break from the real world. "If there's the moonlight, I don't want to wake up from it." The other is Hope World, which he wrote to truly express who he is, followed by P.O.P. (Piece of Peace). A great line from the song is, "Even if you scream your song this world is hard of hearing." It's a song of longing, "I wish I could be piece of peace." Great play on words. Then MOTS:7 was released, and J-Hope graced us with EGO, an infectious song that gets frequent play at my house.

While others in the group haven't released their own mix tapes yet, they have issued singles, worked in conjunction with, or covered songs by other artists. Among those that have touched my heart are

- Winter Bear, Scenery and Sweet Night - V
- Someone Like You - V cover
- We Don't Talk Anymore - Jimin & JK cover
- Nothing Like Us, Lost Stars, If You, Paper Hearts, Purpose, & Falling - JK covers
- Stay Alive - Jungkook w/Suga as producer
- Fools - JK & RM cover
- Promise - Jimin
- 4 O'Clock - V & RM
- Who - Lauv featuring BTS
- Abyss and Tonight - Jin
- I Love You - Jin cover
- Winter Flower - Jounha featuring RM

I could spend hours reviewing/commenting on the songs of BTS from June 2013 until present, but that wasn't the intent and purpose of this book. I simply wanted to show the many ways that BTS and their music touched my life. Earlier I briefly spoke about the uniqueness of their songs, and how so many deviated from the standard pop formula. I've also commented (via my blog), that BTS should no longer be typecast as a mere boy band or be stuck in the K-POP genre—I think they long ago surpassed that. I believe the musical genius of BTS (along with their producers/and co-writers), will find a special place in history. While it's hard to compare greatness throughout the ages, I believe they are one of a kind. Just like Beethoven, Mozart, or The Beatles (and I'm not making any direct comparisons), there will never be another BTS. They each have such depth as individuals and as a team, and in my opinion certainly no other similar group today can stand in their light.

All in all, each member has made an indelible impression on me, whether working in unison with the others, or showing us a more personal side of themselves.

I would be remiss if I didn't mention how BTS inspired me to pick up my guitar again. It had been years since I had done so (after my band broke up), but with the death of my best friend and bandmate Lisa, it was the straw that broke the camel's back. But due to BTS, that spark slowly returned and the first song I learned was V's, Winter Bear. So, thanks guys. It feels good to be back! And Yoongi, it's painful acquiring those calluses, isn't it?

They also turned me onto other performers, and for that I am grateful too.

With all the beautiful songs they keep introducing like, Black Swan, Film Out, Life Goes On, Stigma, Zero O'Clock, and We are Bulletproof: the Eternal, how can we not continue to be inspired by their lyrics, voices, and music?

Jessica's room!

Kai-Ann's early collection. She has double now!

Yoongi in my hobby room

Our IBIS mascot

1st poster in my she shed

ARMY box

Some contents of the box. It's nearly full!

K-POP store shopping spree with Kai-Ann and Jessica

Gift from Wendie

My Christmas gift to IBIS

Besties on Twitter Sept 2021

A bit of Christmas in my office and one of the gifts from Susan F

New pin board

A variation of my ARMY board

ARMY board Christmas 2021

My office

Gift from Pauline made with laser printer

Surprise gift from Ann S

Their Stories

The following section features some of the wonderful stories shared with me on the Discovering BTS website. To retain the feel, intent, (and in many cases respecting the fact that English wasn't their native language), I copied each letter exactly as presented to me. The only exceptions were minor corrections to spelling and grammar simply for clarification's sake, or at the request of certain authors who asked that I edit theirs prior to publication.

It was my idea to make them appear as if they arrived in my mailbox, snail-mailed to me on their own personal stationery.

While a variety of emotions may tug at your heartstrings, make you laugh aloud, or simply smile, most have a common thread that runs through each - the fact that BTS entered their lives at the time when they needed them the most.

I hope you enjoy their heartfelt words as much as I do, and maybe, just maybe, they'll inspire you to give BTS a listen in the future.

Marion

To Samsung Ads and Beyond

I already heard of BTS way back in 2017 when they had a concert here in the Philippines, but I did not pay much attention since I was not into Kpop. Fast forward to 2020, and I was randomly playing YouTube videos while desperately looking for a job online when their Samsung Ad appeared. I enjoyed watching them dancing and singing to Dynamite, then I realized I finished the entire ad! So, I checked the Dynamite MV and I loved it! Since then, I started to watch more random videos until I got hooked all the way!

For me, BTS is not just a music group that performs on stage and makes fans scream and adore them. Their albums are always carefully and intelligently conceptualized. They make music with a purpose and send messages thru their songs. With this, they have united fans from across the globe. I have not known any music act that did the same thing so far. So far, Magic Shop is my comfort song. When I am down, I listen to it then I feel better.

My ultimate bias is Suga because of his unique rapping style and dedication to producing music for the group. I also like his sweet and savage personality. :-) I don't have a specific wrecker because I think the rest of them have already wrecked it hard on me lol! I love all of them individually for different reasons and each of them has a special place in my heart.

They came into my life when I was at my lowest point. Getting to know them has made me less anxious now and made me view life more positively. I learned to accept my weaknesses and limitations. I am so thankful for them coming into my life and I will be with them for as long as it takes.

BTS has taught me how to handle the bashers in real life and how to manage myself in unpleasant situations. Also because of BTS, I feel young again. They bring back my sense of humor that the adulting life has taken away from me. This helps me go on with life.

I embrace their music and support them all the way. I respect their personal lives and will be happy to see them do the things they love on and off cam. My ultimate goal is to watch them live in concert and to sing and dance with them. I want to enjoy that moment with my co-Armies. I am 100% sure, it is one of the biggest highlights of my life. For now, I am happy enough to receive my first merchandise, Winter Package 2021. I hugged the purple pouch as if I'm hugging them. It will always be special to me.

ARMYs, let us continue supporting and loving BTS in any way we can. Thank you to my newly found ARMY friends, both local and abroad. I wish we can get together when the time comes and celebrate our love for our men! Borahae!

Maris15

TO THE PURPLE OCEAN

I didn't know loving yourself was a thing until I found these 7 normal boys from Korea.

I was in 9th at the time I found them, more like THEY FOUND ME! I was a simple introverted girl with not so many friends, I hardly had 2 friends. All the girls in my school including my close friends were so beautiful and cool that everyone would be head over heels for them especially boys. I was not into boys, but I wanted to be cool and beautiful. Looking back, I realize that I was not THAT unfortunate looking. I wanted to be perfect, I wanted to have other's lives, other's face, in short I didn't love what I HAD [except my family]. I was so blind about MY appearance that I didn't see what I had and what I was capable of, since my friends were so busy with their boyfriends [typical teenage stuff].

I was super lonely. One day a classmate of mine began teasing me that everyone was hooked up and I was not [honestly I was not into boys] and then he said that I was still single because my skin was too dark. He made more racist comments and everyone around me was laughing. I was so angry and sad. That day I went home and cried for eternity, I slapped my innocent face for not looking pretty enough and was shouting at myself for not being good enough for my friends and family. I thought I was ugly.

I tried to share my problems with the most trusted well-wishers of my life: my uncle and my mom. They tried to help me with my problems, but even they couldn't heal my wounded heart.

I am very interested in listening to music and one day I was listening to my favorite music channel on TV. And suddenly THIS PARTICULAR KPOP SONG featuring HALSEY played. I liked listening to Halsey, so I gave a listen to this song. I didn't know that this song could change my life forever. It was BTS's Boy with Luv feat Halsey. I was so drawn to their aura that BTS had. And I wanted to know their names. It took me a week to study their names. I slowly started to discover their LOVE YOURSELF albums. Heard many of their speeches, especially Kim Namjoon's speech at the UN.

I began to see myself, love myself and learned to speak myself. Earlier I hated going to school, but after their arrival in my life, I began to be happy. I'm not saying people stopped talking behind my back, but I didn't care because I knew me!

Moreover, I didn't want anyone else to love me because I've got me! BTS made me feel beautiful both inside and

out. And ARMY made me feel that I was included and that I was not an outsider. I started making new ARMY friends and began hanging out with people that had the same purple heart as me. I don't know how to pay them back for making me find me. All I can say is that I would support and love them all equally until my last day on this wonderful purple world. I don't know whether I'll see them or not in real life but I know that they are a big part of my life and existing in the same time as BTS is a blessing! BORAHAE!

MeenuMalu

The Day Time Stood Still - 5/19/19

Hi! let's see how do I start? My name Is Muñeca. (Yes it means Dolly in English.) That's my nickname. But BTS Army Knows me has 엄마 Ladybug (Mama Ladybug). I have two daughters that I call the Ladybugs. That's a different story but I'm here to tell you about my BTS Army experience. I first heard of BTS because the lil ladybug was talking to her friends about how handsome Kookie was and did you know he has my nickname? My usto called me Kookie when I was a baby. That's what she called me, lil Ladybug. She was very excited about this boy name Kookie, so I sat her down and asked her who Kookie was and to invite him over. She was in 4th grade, and I didn't want her to have a boyfriend yet, but I'd like for them to be friends. She started laughing. Mum, Kookie is not in my school. I wish lol. So she had her tablet and showed me the pictures. He belonged to a boy band. Mind you, I just looked at her and said wow, he is so cute, but I didn't have any interest. I just bought her a BTS shirt and that was it. She told me she's been a fan since 2014, when she was 8 yrs old. She said they were teenagers. I totally had no interest. I saw them in a video, and they were so cute dancing, and a school bus came on the screen and I said very cool. But that's what it was in 2016.

In 2017, my lil Ladybug introduced me to the boys again, I was so depressed. That year my big Ladybug graduated from HS and I found myself in the fall with one kid at home and I was worried. One, I'm a very sick human with so many health problems. I have Fibromyalgia, pain 27/7 days a week no cure. I got my diagnosis in 2007. She was a baby, and my big Ladybug has been my ride or died girl. She helped me so much. She made me look like a wonder woman, in the lil Ladybug's eyes. So, she started college. I was like omg, next is the lil ladybug. I'm going to be alone. No more babies. And she took me out of that funk. lil Ladybug helped me see that BTS was there. I started listening to their music looking for translation videos, but I was just there to bond with her. She had a poster that I bought her for having good grades and she was so excited, so she showed me and told me all their names. Mind you I am seeing this poster and looking at their hair and looking at their white clothes and the shoes and I was like this is really cool. And then she told me their names, mind you I'm very bad at names. So, in this poster, Namjoon had blonde hair and the rest of the boys had all black hair and that's why I remembered his name, and she told me it was Rap Monster. I didn't remember the other member's names. And I said to ladybug, they are 7 boys, they are so young they can be my sons. That day she showed me two videos, one was Fire and the other one Mic Drop. I gave them nicknames, so I can learn their names: Rap monster became Mr dimples, Mr Sweetheart is V. Mr Happy is J-Hope. Mr Smiley is Jin. Mr Sweetface is Suga. Mr lips is Jimin, and Mr Sweet Eyes is Jungkook. I was still not on Tweeter my social media for BTS was watching videos on YouTube. Whenever I felt sad i heard this beautiful song Mic Drop.

She went to school one day and that day I was like wow these boys are awesome. Lil by lil I became their fan but how will I be a fan? I'm an old mom. In 2017 I was 40 yrs old 🤭 and whatever, the lil ladybug and I we were just fans and the boys where coming to the BBA. I was so excited for them but still just a fan. They won and I fell asleep. I missed it. But again, nothing much. One day I heard, 'you can't stop me loving myself', and i was like OMG did they just sing, "you can't stop me loving myself" and the lil ladybug said yup mum. They are the sons you always say you needed to love yourself. And that was it, I fell down the rabbit hole, the summer of 2018. Just a fan remember I didn't know what Army was yet bc I wasn't informed or on BTS Twitter. My husband tells us that he got tickets for a concert for BTS. This was after Christmas and I told her, the big Ladybug has to bring you. I can't go. My anxiety and my Fibromyalgia won't let me enjoy it. Then the big ladybug said Mum I can't go either, I have work and campus life is a lot with finals coming. So, I said, I'll take her. For months we were getting prepared, learning their songs from the Wings CD for the first time, and I literally to the day of today, have to stop because I cry when my Mr Happy says Hello Mom 😢💜🐞

It makes me cry.

May 19, 2019, came and I was so nervous because I thought teenagers were going to be all around. What a big surprise. Did I have to tell you that I felt at home and that I felt loved since I entered the stadium? It's an understatement. I got lost and Army helped me. Army was all around and very kind, and no one was saying you don't belong. There were grandparents without their grandkids in this concert. I saw parents with their kids, 40-year-old's too and 50-& 60-year old moms. I still didn't feel I was Army. I got lost going to my seat and I had Rap Monster's jersey of course and the little ladybug had JK's shirt, and this Army said to me who is your bias? Who do you like? And I said well, I don't like them, I love them like they're my own sons. And this Army said, aww look at you, a BTS ARMY Mom. And I was like yeah I could be their mom! 🤣 She had no clue that I had a daughter that is Army. We talked and she went back to her seat, but not before telling me BTS were on Twitter and that's how I found BTS on Twitter. I was surrounded by more Army introducing themselves. It was so cool I was at home at a concert that I didn't want to go because of my fear. And then the boys came, and time stood still. My heart was in love with the sons I wished I had. They made me cry and made be proud when JK flew above us singing euphoria. OMG. I was so proud and a lil bit worried. And the Army behind us was screaming like a devil. She was like, OMGGGGG is he F$#k Flying! Omg, I'm so sorry Mama Ladybug, she apologized during the entire concert. And then the boys sang the last song, Mikrokosmos, and tears just poured more and more. Mind you they were crying themselves. JK and Suga were emotional Suga promised that he'd come back to Met Life stadium again to sing with us. We'll be back Armyyy u see. It was the last time I saw My Sons. And Twitter took me to Batido to praise Japan and S Korea. It was amazing. I have now a BTS Army family. I love all my Moots and I have two BTS Army daughters, one lives in the UK. and the other one lives in the US. They call me Unnie. I have an Army sister in the Philippines. I have my Aussie Army niece, she calls me Mama Bear because I defend BTS and ARMY like hell. I'm a sweet lady but don't mess with my children and my family and don't mess with the Army Noonas. They need love too. I have BTS Army nieces and nephews, and I found my BTS Army Soulmate, yeah Mary. I'm proud to say Army always respects me. I never get drama and the love I share in my tweets is purple love. I'm here to bring joy, the joy that the boys give me. I'm one proud BTS Army Mom bc I belong to the boys who are changing the world. They showed me how to love myself again and be myself, and to never give up. RM made me so proud the day he spoke in the UN. Yeah my head was bigger than my ego! 🤣🤣🤣🐞💜🐞💜🐞 Be proud of who you are. You are BTS Army. Find your rainbow and Be Someone's Rainbow every day. No matter the weather, you will rise up to be an amazing human.

So, if you see my Good morning and Goodnight Moon tweet and you see 🐞💜🐞🐞, that's me your ladybug. I'm studying Korean so i can visit SK one day with the lil ladybug and so I can understand the boys and Kdrama. S Korea has a beautiful culture and is a beautiful country. Can't wait to visit.

🐞💜

The Beginning

I found the field for the BTS Rabbit hole in September of 2019. It was actually the middle of the night, a fateful accident – a measly bored click that changed my life.

First you must know, I used to dance. I did dance for a very long time as a child and through my teens. I did jazz, tap, and ballet – and even dance competitions! I do not dance anymore – teenage attitude and family issues slowly sucked the fun out of that. I do however – like group dancing. Like, a lot.

On that fateful early September morning, I was lying in bed surfing Reddit. I was new to Reddit and my algorithms unknown to us all, a very plain message stared at my face.

"Give it up for their Dancing." Was the cue for me to click. I clicked, thinking, I like dancing right? It took me to BTS music video for Not Today.

I actually remember having a moment of like, "Okay wait, this is BTS. This is Korean. This is bright, and pink, and colorful. Are we sure we want to watch this?"

I watched.

I am so glad I did.

Seconds before the first chorus, when those jackets fly into the air – myself at 3am said aloud "Whoa" alone in my room. It was unlike anything I had seen. I watched the video. Mesmerized by the dancing. I watched it again.

I then listened to the same song over and over. I quickly found Mic Drop, as it was another fast tune and one YouTube music video eventually led me to another. I would stay up for hours and listen to the music, listen to it while I worked, then come home.

About two weeks later, I wanted to learn their names. I wanted to learn their names too of course, figure out who was who, and pinpoint the dance line names. I was able to point out Suga first. I watched factoid videos, funny videos, videos about each boy - I started first by watching the interviews on American Late-Night TV.

I still remember my mind was blown when I found out my bias wasn't a dancer. He didn't take classes like Jimin obviously had; he didn't want to dance - he was a rapper! He made it look so flawless, so easy. And years later we learn he did it all through pain and a hurt shoulder. He's simply amazing.

I am still listening and learning new BTS things today. My official Army day is September 27th. I seriously got into BTS MONTHS after this, perhaps about a year ago (March/April) when I heard Don't Leave Me. Hooked. Done.

I began lurking on Twitter and now almost 2 years later have found another family. BTS is huge on Love Yourself - which is so simple yet one of the hardest things in the world to do. I am learning more about myself, my family, what I think, and mainly - me. I am literally learning to love myself. And I am.

I love my Twitter family. I enjoy seeing their smiles and the happiness they bring me, as the boys bring them.

We are all one. :D

Jessa2727

Yup, Army for Life

Back in December 2016 at the age of 46, my daughter and myself went to visit her online friend from Brazil who was on vacation in Canada. Her friend was a fan of BTS. I had never heard of the group and when she showed me the Blood, Sweat & Tears video, on her phone as we walked through a mall, I said they looked like and sounded like girls and all look the same.

In the beginning of September 2017 my daughter asked me to watch a BTS video. I remember that her friend introduced us to them back in December, but this time I sat down, and I watched it. My daughter was so excited. I noticed that they were really talented. She tried to teach me their names. I decided to surprise her by learning all their names on my own. I jumped down the rabbit hole and have happily lived there ever since. I watched numerous YouTube videos about each member. J-Hope and Rap Monster where the easiest to identify. I wrote notes to help identify the other 5 members. I remember thinking why do they say Jin is the visuals of the group, he is not that good looking. I also had a hard time telling V from Suga. In less than a week after watching countless videos I knew all their stage names and was ordering the presale for Love Yourself Her, on September 4, 2017, from Amazon. When the album arrived on September 18, 2017, I listened to it nonstop, in the car, at work. I could not get enough BTS content. I spent hours on YouTube and Vlive.

My next big step in the fandom was joining Twitter in November 2017 when BTS had 10 million followers. I made my Twitter account @BTSmommy305. I had a picture of BTS as my header and my profile picture. I describe myself as being a wife and a mother but had nothing about my age. I also did not show any pictures of myself. I started following other accounts of older ARMY.

I loved watching VLive, especially "Run BTS", "Bon Voyage ", and I sometimes got lucky enough to catch them live. I would watch them, but not understand what they were saying, with a big smile on my face, and clicking that heart button. Once translations came up I would watch it again. When "The Wings Tour The Final" was going to be live streamed from Korea on VLive I purchased it, and woke up at 3 am on December 9, 2017, to see my first BTS concert live from my bed. It was an emotional concert, I laughed with them and cried with them. I will never forget they sang "Born Singer" then did closing talks. Hobi started crying, then tearier-eyed Tae, followed by crying Jungkook and Yoongi. Jimin was so proud that he didn't cry, Jin had us laughing with his heart hat and finally Namjoon finished up with his inspirational words.

Line Friends opened in NYC, and I went the last week of December 2017. I spent way too much on pillows, stand up dolls and keychains. This was my first time going into NYC to go shopping. I grew up on Long Island, it's a one-hour train ride and I rarely went into the City. BTS changed that.

In April 2018, I was invited to my first GC on Twitter. There were 10 women in this group chat, and we talked every day. They live in the USA, Canada, and Germany. By getting to know them I decided to change my profile picture to one of me and openly spoke about being an over 40 ARMY.

On April 25, 2018, I purchased tickets to the BBMAs, airfare to Las Vegas, and made my hotel reservation. I was going to see BTS perform at the BBMAs with my daughter. I was so excited. It was going to be their comeback stage! We were leaving Friday May 18, the day before my daughter decided she could not go, she did not want to do the flight or be in a crowded venue. So, I decided to go by myself. I knew there were Army activities going on and I am an extrovert, I love meeting new people. So, I went to Vegas by myself and had one of the best vacations of my life. Saturday afternoon wearing my JHOPE shirt I meet up with a group of ARMY and met Trish, we have been friends ever since then. Trish and her daughter were going to the pool, so we parted ways, promising to share an Uber later for an Army dinner at a Korean BBQ. I went walking on the strip. I felt a tap on my shoulder. I turned around and a woman was standing there with a Mang sticker. We started talking, her name was Kim and we hit it off. She came shopping with me than we grabbed a drink at Starbucks. The hours spent with her forged a friendship for life.

My next adventure actually started on May 5, 2018, which was my son's 12th birthday. BTS Speak Yourself tickets went on sale. I had a group of 5 people set up to help me get tickets. I was waiting days before making sure my login worked, then it was time. I had 3 phones, an iPad and a computer set up. Any BTS fan who has tried to get tickets knows the little walking man and over 1,000 people in front of you. I was so upset waiting my turn knowing they would sell out fast. Tears were running down my face in frustration thinking I will not get in. Than one of my friends, Linsey from work, got me GA (floor standing room) for the September 28, 2018, Prudential center in NJ and I got us upper balcony seats for the 9/29. Now my tears were tears of joy, I am seeing my first full live in person BTS concert.

NYC Army were doing a get together in Time Square on June 9, 2018, for BTS' 5th anniversary. It was on the red stairs in Time Square, right near Line Friends store. While at Line Friends I got the attention of a JTBC journalist who asked if she could interview me at my house for a BTS special. The special was aired in Korea on July 5, 2018, and I got my two minutes of fame on TV.

On September 28 and 29, 2018, my daughter and I saw BTS at the Love Yourself concert, Prudential Center in NJ. Some people spent a week camping out online for GA wrist bands. I got up at 4 am it was dark and raining, I was one of the first non-campers online. I got number 838 at 12:30 pm. We got a standing spot off the corner of the stage. It was all I dreamed of. The concert was an incredible experience. The next day I got up at 5 am for merch. I got the last group picket. We were the first row of the second section. Loved it so much, you could see all the choreo.

With the help of friends, I was lucky enough to get tickets to Citifield for BTS's first stadium concert in the US and it was GA again. This time I went with five of my Twitter group chat friends. We had a great spot on the left of the center stage, and I was also able to walk to front of the main stage. I can't explain what amazing concerts BTS put on.

Love Yourself Speak Yourself was announced and I was fortunate in getting tickets for Day 1 Chicago and both days in New Jersey. A friend that I met at BBMA in 2018, invited me to join her on Day 2 floor seats in Chicago. Went by myself to Chicago and met with my twitter GC friends. May 11th was a cold day with rain on and off, went with Trish to the pop-up shop spent several hours online and made new Army friends. Trish and I had floor seats to the right of the center stage, and yes Soldier Field is bloody cold. Luckily the rain had stopped. JK flew over us, the show exceeded all expectations. The next day it was cold and rainy the whole concert. This time I was on the left of center stage. BTS gave us another incredible show even with the weather conditions.

The next BTS concerts I went to were May 18th and 19th in New Jersey at MetLife Stadium. Went with my daughter and was in the 300s day 1 and 200s day 2. My husband asks, how you can see the same concert so many times. The reason why, ever BTS concert is different. The energy from Army, the excitement of each song, when will we cry, when will we laugh, and can I do this every day for the rest of my life.

I finally meet my first local Army in August 2019, my Unnie Christine, instant friends and have spent many hours talking about BTS and sharing of lives with each other. The first weekend after we met, we had a great time going to a cup event in NYC for JK's birthday.

The following week I asked a friend from middle school, who is not army to join me for another cup event in NYC. She had fun but still isn't army. My friends and family don't get BTS, my daughter who is ARMY, accepts that I am obsessed with BTS.

With 2019 coming to a close, I decided to try to get tickets to Jingle Ball in LA to see BTS one more time. I got a 4th row seat to the right of the stage. Another solo trip which I loved. Vacations with Army are the best. Had lunch at Chosungalbee, visited Line Friends LA, saw BTS close up, went namjooning at the Getty Center, and walks on Manhattan Beach.

I live in NY so you would think I would do Time Square for New Year's Eve. To see BTS one last time, but my family did not want me to go, and I just saw them up close at Jingle Ball. So, I stayed with my family and friends.

Wow, MOTS world tour for 2020 was announced and I got presale with my Weverse membership. I purchased silver sound check for both days in NJ; one gold sound check in Chicago; and great 100 section for day 2 Chicago. My dreams have come true I will finally get sound check.

Then COVID. BTS postponed their concerts, but I am so happy I still have my tickets. They keep me going thinking one day I will get to see them, and I have sound check. Watched online concerts, spent hours on Twitter, VLive, YouTube, and Weverse. Life Goes On, Dynamite, Butter, Hot 100 number 1 Grammy nomination. Bought so much merch on Weverse that you would think I would be a stockholder by now.

As soon as our household was vaccinated I spent a week in Las Vegas with my BTS Army friend I met 3 year earlier at BBMA. Trish, Kim, and I were reunited after seeing each other last at the May 2019, Love Yourself Speak Yourself concert in NJ. I had a great time walking around casinos, sharing meals, watching BTS on Billboard Music awards, and the Grand Canyon.

I was devastated when Ticketmaster refunded my MOTS tickets but lucky to be able to go see Permission to Dance Live in LA. No, I didn't get great seats, but I was able to get tickets and this time my daughter joined me. I really can't believe I spent a week in LA from November 26 to December 3, 2021. It feels like a lifetime ago and it hasn't even been a month when I am writing this. Since I was on EST I found it easy to get up at 5 am on 11/27 for merch. I called my ARMY friends that I was meeting up with to find out if they wanted any merch. I bought for myself, my daughter and 6 other friends. I enjoyed seeing BTS four times with army, we laughed, we cried, they made us so happy and BTS looked so happy. I am looking forward to traveling to see BTS and fellow ARMYs for years to come.

BTSMommy305

I "Broke the Silence"

I watched YouTuber Ryan Higa's short films with actress Arden Cho, including Every Romantic Movie and Agents of Secret Stuff (ASS). Since I thought she was clever and funny, I looked up her Vlog. A follower asked her favorite BTS song, and she said Blood, Sweat, and Tears.

I had seen a lot of kdramas, but I hadn't been impressed by other kpop songs (except Dum Dum by Red Velvet). Since I liked Arden Cho, I watched B,S,& T - and was blown away!

It was so sexy it made me blush, but the level of artistry was unlike anything I'd ever seen before. There was so much more to learn after that first viewing, and the first thing I wanted to know was the names of Tae and Jin and the significance of their climactic scene.

As I learned more about Jin, I came across solo stans who thought he should leave the band, so I began learning about the other members with caution, to find out if they treated Jin with respect. By watching lots of YouTube videos, I learned how much all the members cared about each and complemented each other in both skills and personality. Once I joined Twitter, I realized that "OT7" was the only way. When I found that I was willing to fiercely defend attacks on any of the members - by solo stans, the media, or the uninformed gp

(general public: non-ARMYs) I began to call myself ARMY.

At the same time, I was learning about their music. I heard a violin cover of DNA, which had come out recently, and found performance videos of DNA and Mic Drop. I had never really listened to rap music, and I was very surprised that the band who created BST and DNA also made something as harsh and boastful as Mic Drop! I let it slide, though, as I discovered other melodic songs with deep meaning - and ties to the BTS Universe - like Spring Day, Serendipity, Awake, I Need You, and "Butterfly".

The unusual structure and sounds in BTS music often puzzled me at first. I was used to radio pop music, and I had learned more about rock music over the years. I loved classical, big band, early jazz, show tunes, folk songs, bluegrass, and anything with acapella harmonies. I found that BTS music drew from all these sources, and in addition edm (I didn't even know what edm was before BTS), hip hop, rap, and smooth r & b.

BTS changed the way I listened to music. When I read the translated lyrics of their songs, their effect on my heart multiplied, and I began to truly love music that would never have appealed to me before.

I even learned to enjoy the amazing lyricism and multi-lingual wordplay of their harshest rap songs. I became less afraid of anger; of speaking up for and defending myself and others.

The international fandom of ARMY made me more tuned in to world news and cultures. It was the first time since I was a child that I really felt I could just enjoy the company of black friends without the wall of the history of slavery and divided social networks almost palpable between us. The tolerance, respect, and celebration of all lgbtq+ incarnations helped me have compassion when my son told me he was a girl. Lgtbq+ ARMYs became helpful resources. I even found friends whose families had similar mental health and physical disability struggles.

I didn't tell anyone outside of my family about my interest in (obsession with?) BTS for the first year. BTS were too young, sexy, and attractive for a woman my age to fangirl. I was too old to fan"girl" anything!

Now am proud of my affection for these courageous young men and feel blessed to be the first in my peer group to have discovered them.

My friends nod and roll their eyes as I incorporate BTS into almost every conversation.

(BTS are so active and have such a broad range that it is easy to do). One friend wouldn't let me talk about them at all. He had seen them on carpool karaoke and decided he was "not interested." An intelligent man, a friend, a lover of music, had dismissed my good opinion entirely, performance unheard and unseen. That was my most painful moment as an ARMY. Neither I, nor my husband (who considers himself a "casual" BTS fan) can understand the ridiculous, unfounded prejudices against BTS - even the ones that led me, myself, to hide my fangirling for a whole year! I am fortunate to have gotten past my prejudices. Now I'm just waiting for the rest of the USA to catch up!

Peach

Bangtan Sonyeondan:
How 7 artists from Korea
helped me discover myself

It was a sunny day in April 2021 - summer break. Both my parents were at work, and I was lazing around, surfing the internet. Being a music lover, I would often listen to music while doing assignments, and just about all the time. I found a random playlist on Spotify and listened to it. Many known songs came and went by. Suddenly, a song came on and started with a sweet, expressive voice that seemed familiar. I closed my eyes and vibed to the whole song, without even understanding it - and at the end of it, I was stunned. Little did I know that the band who sang that song, would one day help me discover and be myself.

My journey with BTS actually began way before I even became a fan. In 2018, during the LY era, one of my best friends (who isn't my friend anymore), was an ARMY. She would obsess about their songs all day long, due to which a few of their hit songs (Idol, Fake Love, etc) got stuck in my head. However, I wasn't a fan. I found some songs good. Casually listened to them. I didn't hate/dislike them but didn't follow them. I didn't even know all the members' names (I can't even imagine)!

Fast forward to summer break, 2021. The news that our final exams (scheduled to be held that May) were going to be canceled due to the pandemic, had just come out. My mind weighing heavy with mixed feelings, I put away all my tenth-grade books and... didn't know what to do next. The past two years, I'd drawn up an extensive plan of what I was going to do in the 11th and 12th grades, to secure my dreams of working in the technology sector. All of a sudden, now that the exams were canceled without any notice, I had no idea what to do. My mind was blank. Computer Science was my passion, a field I'd been wanting to get into since the 2nd grade! But I'd felt like I'd lost all sense of what I had to do next. Preparing for college, learning new programming languages, building my resume, all that seemed far-fetched for me now.

I'd been bullied and spent at least a year with no friends in middle school. Since then, I've suffered from severe body image issues and bouts of anxiety. I'd begin and end harmful diets, even exercise to the point of breathlessness, all to hate how I looked in the end. It seemed like there was no end to this cycle. Small and insignificant comments that people made, would affect me so badly. One such incident happened when I visited my cousin's house in May 2021. My aunt casually remarked that my face had gotten rounder and swiftly moved on to a different topic. She probably spent a few seconds saying that one sentence and didn't mean much, but you know how long it stayed in my head? Two weeks.

A few days after that, I looked at my face in the mirror and just felt like punching the mirror. I managed to calm myself down and thought of going for a walk to clear my mind. As I walked out the door, my mom said that my face was looking a little puffy. I slammed the door and as I walked down the stairs, tears started streaming down my face. I stopped and slid to the ground and proceeded to cry for the next fifteen minutes. Why was I crying? Not because of what my aunt said two weeks ago, not because of what my mum said. I cried because of what I said to myself. I hated that I was the one who hated myself, so much. That day, I went over all the worst things I ever said to myself, and one thought kept going in my head - "why me?" "Why do I hate myself so much?"

I was listening to my playlist while crying when Jin's solo Epiphany from the Love Yourself album came on. His soulful voice singing "I'm the one I should love…" just struck a chord in my heart. I went home that day, with red eyes and a puffy face (classic aftermath of crying), but a weight lifted off my head and heart.

That is ultimately how I was motivated to listen to their music. First, I fell in love with their beautiful voices, tasteful rapping and excellent music. Then came all the Bangtan Bombs, VLives, Run BTS episodes, etc. From just wanting to know the names of the seven members, I became a loyal ARMY.

Once I started to listen to their discography, I truly realized the power of their music. Every album, song of theirs, had me feeling strong emotions and really rekindled my love for myself as well as for my passions and the people around me. After my rough year in 7th grade, I went from an active, confident, extroverted kid to someone with not even an ounce of self-confidence. Someone who hated herself more than anything. Someone who would do anything to be born as another person.

Bangtan, how can I thank you? You helped me discover myself and really, truly love myself for who I am. The songs on all their Love Yourself albums helped me more than I can ever express with words. I found myself gaining more confidence in myself, my abilities and also exploring the things I was really good at. I started playing the guitar and singing again (after a break), and really loved it. I started participating in more activities at school, signing up for more things, really breaking out of the shell I'd built for myself. I also started eating more balanced foods, and still enjoyed the junk food I liked - in moderate quantities. I started exercising regularly, not because I had to, but because I wanted to. I also started learning Korean and learning more about their culture (not just for BTS), but to also expand my horizons and skillsets. As of October, I progressed past the beginner level, and I couldn't be prouder!

Magic Shop and Mikrokosmos made me feel like I wasn't alone, RM's mix tape Mono and JHope's mix tape Hope World, were for those days that I wanted to feel calmer and more centered. Suga's mix tapes were for the days I felt fierce and ready to take on anything. Seoul, Boy in Love, Wishing on a Star, Dimple when I just want to vibe to music. Idol, I Need U, Fire, Dope, MIC Drop, Blood Sweat and Tears, Fake Love, Boy with Luv, Butter, Telepathy, DNA - for when I was energetic and felt like dancing. Permission to Dance, Dynamite for making me happy at the end of a long school week. Their debut album for when I wanted to listen to hardcore hip hop. And finally, We Are Bulletproof - the Eternal and Young Forever, for when I wanted to be motivated and work hard. Their albums 'BE' (special mentions - Telepathy, Life Goes On) and 'Map of the Soul 7' (special mentions - Moon, ON) were absolutely wonderful. I can't wait to listen to all the songs they're gonna put out next. Their music means so much to me.

As time went on, I realized that it wasn't just their music that helped me. Their personalities, their journeys continue to motivate me. Whenever I'm lazy and don't feel like doing something, I remind myself that hard work truly brings rewards. They're also some of the most genuine artists I have ever seen. Their journey from rookies to world stars, all while remaining humble kings, is more than inspiring. Through becoming a member of ARMY, I also found a huge group of like-minded people, with similar goals, all inspired to be a better version of ourselves.

To all those people saying the ARMY is a crazy fandom, please think again. All fandoms are a little crazy, but true ARMY are the fans who love and support BTS but don't spread hate elsewhere. I found a new best friend (also ARMY) and became closer with an older friend (also ARMY), and I couldn't be more thankful for them. They are now the people I can share every little sorrow and happiness with. We motivate each other.

I'm not going to say that I completely love myself and that now I never doubt myself because I still do. The difference now is that I know how to learn from any mistakes and move on. I'm also discovering more about myself on my journey to self-love. Thank you to the person whose random playlist I listened to on Spotify that brought me here. As we often say in this fandom, "don't be upset if you didn't find BTS in their earlier days. You found them when you needed them the most."

I really hope that one day I get to experience their music live, in concert. More than any picture or autograph, I want to just let them know how much they helped. With everything going on with me and with millions of others.

This last paragraph might sound a little cringe, but it's from the bottom of my heart. Thank you to my parents for not caring when I randomly break out into BTS dances, my friends for helping me be sane and loving this beautiful group with me, and finally - Namjoon, Jin, Hobi, Taehyung, Jungkook, Jimin and Yoongi (and Bang PDnim for the start of it all!). For all the inspirational words, genuine moments, crazy laughs, and absolutely wonderful music. If you're reading this, I'm gonna be with you till the end of time. If BTS ever ends as a band, I'll still be here. Part of ARMY, with you on this journey forever.

Shreya_005

Depression and a Debt of Gratitude

My daughter took care of my mom after she got sick. After her passing, my daughter suffered from severe depression. A few days of feeling lost and unsure of where to go from there, she was mindlessly searching for something to watch and came across a Kdrama, which just so happened to mention BTS. She did some research and fell for them immediately. I did my own research on them and found so much hate directed at them. For the safety of my daughter's mental health, I had to find out more about them. Once I found out how incredible their music and lyrics were, I started to help try to get "Make It Right" played on our local radio, with barely any results. A few short months later, on Christmas Day, my girls' dad passed away. On the night of his death, suddenly our radio station played "Make It Right", 4 times in a 6-hour period. My girls are convinced their dad, who had jokingly teased them about listening to their music, was trying to send them a message through BTS.

BTS has truly been a source of comfort for our entire family. A light at the end of a dark tunnel. Their lyrics are so moving and have helped give us all strength. In a year and a half, we lost 3 close family members, plus add the lock down from the pandemic. I'm positive I would be telling a completely different more devastating story had it not been for my daughter finding BTS when she did. I owe them a huge debt of gratitude!

Whispering2t

My summer vacation (with BTS) –
From a high school math teacher,
a new Army member

Every dark cloud has a silver lining;
Covid-19 is the current dark cloud in
our life, but there is a silver lining that
gave me a joyful summer vacation. Being
a high school teacher, every break is very
important; especially, a long summer
vacation is a big part of enjoyment for
most teachers. I'd been traveling every
summer until last year but stopped
because of Covid-19. Last summer I didn't
feel that bad staying home and thought
it was just a temporary thing. However,
we were wrong. Before my summer break,
my husband and I had been talking back
and forth to decide whether we were going
on a trip or not, but then thought about
all the new variants and decided to stay
home. I was disappointed, depressed, and
wondering how and what I was going to
do during my 2-month vacation. Thank
God who opened a window for me. I
joined the BTS fan club about a week into
my summer break, which was the best
thing I did this summer. I'd heard about
BTS and was also influenced by my
former principal who retired, but never
thought about joining the Army club. To
be honest, I'm a hard-headed person
about being a star chaser and I had never
joined any fan club. BTS' fan club is my
first one and is probably going to be the
last one for being a star chaser since
they're my stars that I love so much; their
music brought me happiness and a joyful
summer.

I've learned a lot about the special team BTS and have enjoyed watching and listening to all the BTS MVs. I'm amazed how in the world, everyone is inspired and engaged by their powerful music. I wish I could engage my students like them. I have to say BTS can also be described as Best Team Spirit. While I was catching up on everything BTS has done in the past 8 years, I was wondering how I could have missed the best artist music in 8 years; I must have been very busy with my job. The first month I'd been watching all their MVs, and I'd like to share some of my thoughts:

BTS is the best because when you watch their MV or listen to their songs, you can feel it. Their music is very inspirational, engaging, and empowering and they sing and dance with their hearts and emotions. They go all out and try very hard to bring the world a peaceful, joyful, and wonderful life, bring spiritual support, and bring us life motivation and energy. They are not just artists and musicians, but also God-like and geniuses because their music unites our world. You can get feelings and emotions even if you don't understand the language of the song. Their dance is full of energy and emotion. Their music can heal your pain and troubles. I became a fan not because of their fame, but because of their humanity and personalities. The seven artists are seven angels to their fans; they try very hard to connect to them with their very busy schedule through a variety of media such as VLive, Weverse, etc. Each of them has their own talent, personality, and

uniqueness that were chosen by God to match very well to make this team so special.
They are brothers who help and take care of each other. When I was watching documentaries Behind the Scenes, Run, and BTS in the Soop, etc., I was strongly wondering if they were raised by the same parents. There is one word that can describe the feeling of my heart when I watch their show and touching tears fill my eyes.

The seven brothers as I observed: RM is a smart, talented, and compassionate leader, Jin is multi-capable with a special voice artistry, Suga swags with confidence and talent, Jimin is very sophisticated, affectionate, warm-hearted, sympathetic, and kind, J-Hope is a ray of sunshine on top of the world, V is uniquely talented and attractive, Jungkook is driving, dynamic, lively, and spirited. They are all very handsome in their own way that drives their fans crazy. Their singing, dancing, and every bit of action are immersed in our hearts, bringing us many beautiful feelings, and yearning and love for life. They work very hard and are rich, but they share their wealth to help locally and internationally. While I was trying to learn all about them, I found out they donated a good amount of money. They support UNICEF and donate money monthly. Their stretch far exceeds the realm that their age can reach. Their artwork can heal your sadness and bring you happiness and hope. The way they deliver their music does not have a language difficulty because you can feel it. Their music doesn't separate ethnic, gender and age so everyone can enjoy it. This is why they united our world and their fandom is all over the world. I'm very proud to be an Army member and will continue to support and follow them.

Last but not least, thank you for being the silver lining in the current Covid dark cloud; thank you BTS for all you do for our world; thank you for your amazing work and keep up the fantastic work. Thank you so much Bang PD the father of BTS for developing such an outstanding and talented team.
Please remember you're always in your Fandom's hearts. Be safe, healthy, and take good care of yourselves because the world needs your joyful music to bring happiness.

Guang-Yin Swanland

We Find Them When We Need Them The Most

It all started because of a YouTube video where YouTubers reacted to kpop and the first song they heard was dope by BTS. I searched the song and I kinda liked it but I was not pulled into the fandom. Then after a year I saw mic drop on my tv and I absolutely loved it and added it to my shower playlist, but again I didn't know much about them. It was finally in 2019 that I again came across a YouTube video where this girl was singing the chorus of DNA and it was stuck in my head and I was like I need to listen to this song. After that I felt like I was on an inclined plane and I knew i was gonna fall hard. 2019 the year I became an army was the worst year of my life (actually, 2020 was the worst) as I had faced my first failure and my dreams were crushed. I couldn't make it to a medical college I started hating myself more and more. I blamed myself for everything and I felt like this self-hatred was killing me from inside, but then songs like love myself and magic shop really helped me a lot. Their songs are very powerful and meaningful. Music has always been my healer and me becoming an army when I was absolutely broken makes me feel like they are my angels. I'm trying to love myself more every day and I truly want to thank BTS for making music which are so meaningful. They are my hope, my light, my BTS.

Bhavya 101

Army With Love

Beginning of 2019 was a rough year for me. I was going through job transitions and struggling mentally with who I was as a person and where I was going in my early 20s. I remember seeing a post somewhere of Boy With Luv and I decided to check it out. I have no idea what it was, but I saw those bright smiles and happy colors and I instantly fell in love. Suddenly, all the darkness I had seen for the past few months in 2019 was just gone and I remembered just singing to that song day after day after day until I discovered more of BTS. Well, almost two years later and here I am preaching about BTS 24/7. Even today, on my darkest days, I watch a video of them laughing and suddenly all my worries, fears, and anxieties are all out the window. I love the message they send. I love that they care so much. Thank you, BTS <3

tori_edits

To the boys who played by different rules

There's an old saying, we don't always know what we want, but we can be sure we don't like what we don't know. When we get pleasure from something, it's not based on what we see, hear, or feel. Instead, it's based on what we believe that thing to be.

I didn't start listening to BTS until much later. The first time I heard their song, I was mesmerized. It reminded me of bright summers and the evening rain, things that were not and everything that should be, endless conversations and loyal friends, guilt and love. It was a song about nothing, yet it had everything I needed to hear. A simple song with the least complicated story. Why did I like it? Maybe it was my story too. It took me 3 days to ultimately be a fan. An ARMY. It was a little bit like magic.

When I first started listening to BTS, I was in a bad place emotionally and physically. I was barely hanging on. Everything seemed so bleak that I would sometimes feel like it hurt to be alive. It hurt to breathe. It hurt to be me. Even the good things that happened to me did not cheer me up.

When I first started watching their songs, it felt like eating chocolate, like having hot soup when feverish. I had many problems, but I felt their music lifted the burdens when listening to their songs. I didn't obsess over the issues I couldn't solve, but I was living in the moment. I don't speak Korean, so even though I appreciated their angelic voices, I did not understand save for a few English words peppered in the lyrics. I slowly wondered what the songs meant. I looked it up online and to my immense surprise, the lyrics resonated with me. They began to mean more to me. Because I now understood. It felt like someone understood me.

Little by little, my mental health improved, even my mother noticed. They inspired me. To do better, to be me and love myself. When things seemed challenging, I found myself relying on BTS to help me. I would start my day with a song, end my day watching their interviews or fun content. Listening to their songs gave me strength and peace. It felt like someone was reassuring me that everything was going to be okay.

I absolutely loved their songs, but I never discussed them with anyone else because I was tired of explaining that I didn't like them for their looks. I even went as far as hiding the songs in my Spotify playlists. My favourite songs were the ones I never talked about, the ones I listened to on repeat in secret, the ones I had hidden away.

Later when I saw performances from Beatles, Michael Jackson and Freddy Mercury and watched the crowd go wild at their concerts, I felt like I missed out on that experience. But BTS is happening here now, and one day I might be able to go to their concerts. I don't want to miss out on enjoying their music or wait for 20 or 30 years for people around me to catch on about how wonderful they are. Then I realized that I shouldn't have to hide my love for BTS because of some insensitive comments. How could I have ever hidden away my love for BTS?

I learned a lot from them.

Namjoon taught me unparalleled leadership skills. Seokjin taught me to be confident no matter what.

Yoongi taught me to keep my cool in the face of trouble.

Hoseok taught me to be optimistic no matter what, and that hope is our greatest weapon.

Taehyung taught me that it's okay to mess up sometimes; it's no big deal.

Jungkook taught me that no one is born good at everything. We have to work for it.

Jimin taught me the best way to get a good friend is to be one yourself.

I also want to thank them for making my life better. At the end of a long day, I found comfort in their music, their fun games, watching them cook, their dance, and all kinds of content. A good song would put a smile on my face in no time. Watching my favourite Run BTS episodes, just listening to my favourite songs, trying my hand at cooking, these were the few things that kept me going.

In the wise words of John Keating from Dead Poets Society:

Medicine, law, business, engineering are noble pursuits and necessary to sustain life. But poetry, beauty, romance, love, these are what we stay alive for.

tiredladki

A Not So Special, Special Story

I don't think I have a big story of how I became an army, but for me it will always be special.

I remember it was when I was at one of the lowest points of my life, both mentally and physically. I have a skin condition called "Atopic Dermatitis" and I was going through a really bad flare up. My health kept deteriorating and nothing seemed to be going my way. My mental health was in a really bad state too and everything around me just made me so sad.

I always knew about BTS and had heard a few songs too but never got invested as a fan before.

But for some reason, this time, even amidst all my pain, something about them called out to me. I remember one day out of nowhere, my curiosity took control of me and I wanted to learn their names, so I took my very first step towards the "rabbit hole".

I searched for their names, their videos, their music, and I found myself smiling again, I felt happy. Their videos were the only thing that could make me smile at that time and as I went deeper and deeper into their music and the lyrics, as I learned more about their personalities, the messages they wanted to convey, the more I fell in love.

I've been an army for a year and a half now and I've truly enjoyed every moment of it. I've learned so much about life, about love, about happiness, about what it means to be a better person not only for yourself but for the people around you, and I have both BTS and ARMY to thank for it all.

Thank you BTS for coming into my life, I will always regret not finding you sooner but my love for you which might've started late, will continue on forever 💜

Jooniebot

The Dream

Some may find it weird, or some may find it freaky, or something drawn from a book, but it is all real. I discovered BTS during the most critical time in my life; so critical it felt as though I was thrown into an abyss down to the lowest point of my life. So bad that it brought me into depression and anxiety. I grew up loving music (played piano since I was 7) and used that to alleviate any emotional pain I go through, but that time, nothing - not even my favorite 90's hits or Christian melodies took away the pain. Telling people that I was in despair was an understatement. I needed a remedy — and fast before I loose myself. Then a dream occurred.

But before I write about the dream let me put my story in a bit more context. During the time I was going through difficulties in my life, I only know of BTS. I see their posters taped on my daughter's wall, which I don't really pay attention to. I hear the boy band's name mentioned a lot by my cousin who's an army since they debuted, but again, I never paid attention. I am one of those people who don't want to put a little effort to know names and faces, and yes I have to admit I once said, "they all look alike." I am one of those people who just turn my ears the other way around and leave the moment I hear "BTS". There was no way I would get into another boy band, especially kpop since I retired from boy bands back in the early 2000 (gives away the idea of how old I am… bwahahaha).

Now let me tell you about the dream. It was so vivid; I wrote it down the following day the dream occurred. It started out with me checking into a Bed and Breakfast for a few days to get away from the chaos of life. I wanted some peace and quiet time. After setting down my luggage in the room, I grabbed a book and headed downstairs to do some reading in one of the huge living rooms (there were two across each other).

I settled down on a comfortable couch and started reading when all of a sudden I heard loud noises right outside the window. There were people running around screaming and peeking through the windows. I thought, "what in the world is going on?" A staff came by, so I asked what the chaos is all about. She said, "someone found out that a famous boy band is staying in our Bed and Breakfast." She left and I looked around to see who it was. Right across the living room from where I was sitting were guys laughing and joking around. I couldn't make up any of their faces, except for J-hope (I didn't know who he was at that time). Then all of a sudden someone jumped from behind the couch and sat next to me. I looked at him and asked, "And who are you? What's your name?" He answered, "Hi! I'm Jungkook," with his right arm stretched out for a handshake. I shook his hand and said, "nice to meet you." After that introduction, I looked across the living room where the rest of the group was still hanging out, laughing, and making jokes. I then saw another glimpse of J-hope before waking up.

I thought it was weird that they appeared in my dream, because I don't even know who is who. A few weeks after that dream, I wandered into my daughter's room and started examining the photos and faces. I couldn't recognize who Jungkook was since they all had different hairstyles and color. So I asked my daughter who Jungkook is. She pointed to him, but again, he didn't look like the guy in my dream. Then she pointed to another photo: this one specifically …

… and that blew me away! That's exactly how he looked like in my dream. That's the guy who introduced himself! The rest was history.

I started learning their names, then watched cracks on YouTube, but what drew me to them is their music.

Music has once again given me the chance to heal, thanks to BTS. They are my companions when I go on long drives while I clear my mind or cry out my fears and worries. Their music keeps me company when I journal or when I do chores. When I started learning their songs and their meaning, it dug down deep in my heart to the point where my worries would be erased and "life goes on."

Now I am a solid army (although a baby army), whose biases are Jungkook and Taehyung - and the rest of the members are wreckers - but still love them all. Thanks to their music, the way they make me laugh, the way they let me forget my problems, fears and anxieties, their genuine personalities that we can relate to and their love and care for us armies regardless of how long we've been one. The timing was impeccable… discovering them through a dream could not have come at a more perfect time.

ShookieNuna

My Untold Story

Hiiii BTS

I am sitting by the window thinking about what exactly to write, not because I don't know what to write but because I have soo much to say that I don't know where to start. My words cannot express the feelings so I wish there was a way I could express all my feelings in one word, but I guess that's impossible. My name is Arzoo which means wish/desire. I was born in May 2000 in a small town in north Pakistan, I have two sisters, both who are proud ARMYs too like me and one younger brother. I spent seven years in that beautiful town surrounded by nature and mountains, I would wake up to the chirping of birds every morning and of course to the annoying rooster. We had many deep rivers and lakes and so I grew to love swimming.

In 2008 we moved from that beautiful small town to the UK. I joined a new school; however, it was really hard to get along with the children as the languages we spoke we're totally different. I was a goofy child and grew up with many male cousins therefore I was very boyish. I went through bullying as I was different, but I got through as I didn't understand what they said, but I understood their mocking laughter.

I grew to be hated by people because they saw me as different - they saw how boyish I was and once they learned my name, they would laugh and say you mean the yogurt, (my real name is Pakiza which means pure and there happens to be a yogurt company that goes by the same name). Therefore, I prefer the name Arzoo instead, which I named myself cos it means wish. I wished people would see me for who I was and then I wish that they accepted my name. Some would call me cow because of the yogurt company logo. I once had girls come up to me and said I saw you on the weekend and I asked where, and they laughed and said on the yogurt box - we saw the cow. But today, I'm not going to shy away from the fact that all this happened - this is still part of my identity, I am now confident in who I have become, I have accepted my past mistakes and like you said RM...I finally did it! Today I spoke myself!

As a child I had anger issues and I fought with everyone. When I changed schools I once again was bullied, every time I sat in a seat, the person next to me would always move away, and I saw how they secretly looked at each other and then would glance at me and laugh. During this time, I lost my beloved Uncle to whom I was really close to. During this time, all my confidence had drained and my happiness there was none. I grew so annoyed at everything that when someone would talk to me I wouldn't care. I started to become mischievous and would cause chaos in the classroom. I started to disrespect the teachers as they didn't see what I went through and every day my dad would get a phone call of complaint, saying they would suspend me. Thinking back, I realize how crazy I was 😄. Later that year I lost another close beloved person - my granddad passed away and so once again, I grew quite again. I am writing this, and I am crying. I started to lose focus in school and was really behind, then I stopped doing schoolwork altogether and would get shouted at in school because all my life has been a failure, so I knew nothing was going to go right. I saw how much I had changed, and it hurt to know that I was once the girl who loved to go out and enjoy adventures, yet this version of myself I lost, upon moving to the UK. My experience moving abroad changed me, I hated going out, I grew anxious at the thought of meeting and facing people. But one day I sat quietly in my room crying cos I was denied a place in college. My sister was in the same room and watching some silly tiktoks, and I saw V. He was doing something funny, and it made me laugh, at my most vulnerable moment, while I was crying. At that moment my heart was filled with so much awe at V and he's healing smile - I continued watching BTS tiktok edits with her and saw so many comments from people calling themselves ARMYs and I was surprised as to what exactly that meant. I saw just how everyone in the comments were so content and happy at being you're fans and at that moment I knew I had found my safe place, that I now proudly call my second home and family. Knowing how the 7 of you were far from home too, dealing with hate and yet still working so hard and proving the haters wrong, I began to connect with you as it mirrored very much my own personal situations.

I started to search for songs by BTS and came across the perfect song 'The truth untold' this song reminded me that I wasn't alone in what I was going through, when I heard this song it felt like it was written for me. It clicked so well with my life as if you knew what I was going through.

After listening to many songs and as I got to know all of you, I started to feel connected to you and found that all my happiness lay within the seven of you. As I got to know you all, I realized how much I liked and got connected to RM - because of how he took care of the members even when they don't notice and how beautiful he looked when he smiled, and I saw that you all worked hard and yet smiled and so I realized how much I had ahead of me. I thought how one day you were normal people and so I grabbed courage and told my dad I wanted to continue with education that I gave up on. I studied a year course in teaching and now I will soon receive my diploma, teaching children and young people in schools and colleges. Then I will study two more years of teaching and training, then I will soon start to teach.

Moving from sad stuff, I am now 20 years old and now I am settled and content with everything, I now live with scars from back home in north Pakistan, scars of mountains that I fell on when I was hiking, to a scar on my lip that a child once gave me in a fight. I also have a Harry Potter scar on my forehead from when I fell off a roof when I was little. I am glad I am alive cos I now have BTS, and Army and I enjoy everything that you prepare for us. I enjoy all your songs, but my fav is Mikrokosmos cos this song touches my heart and is the only song that made me dance (I never dance). I also like black swan, no more dream and fire, and the list will go on - I just love all your songs!!

I really enjoy being an army and I am glad that we (army) have you seven birds of hope. We all love you and I hope you achieve more than what you dream. I hope we can meet one day although it's impossible as I live very far, throwing my Purple love to you, so please catch onto it.

P.S. RM I saw when you are really happy you smile with your teeth and it's soo cute ;) Continue smiling! 💜🤗

Love from across the world,
yours truly Pakiza/Arzoo

Namjoon...Taehyung...Yoongi

I Just Wanted to Learn Their Names

My name is Gail, and I became an "ARMY" around the time Dynamite came out, I was walking past my daughter's room, she became an ARMY after One Direction broke up, she was playing Dynamite. I stuck my head into her room and asked her who was singing.

They are a Korean Group named BTS, I was like oh really? I closed her door and came downstairs opened my laptop and typed in BTS, I was just curious as to who they were and their names, that was it.

I went to YouTube and started watching their videos, then I started to learn more and more about them, and before you knew, I became "ARMY". I didn't realize that I was actually considered a "Noona", at first I felt kind of cringy being an "older woman" who could very well be one of their moms. (Oh God did I just say that out loud?).

After about a few weeks I had fallen down the rabbit hole and fell head over heels in love with them. I am a recovering alcoholic and was struggling. They say you find BTS when you need them the most, they ended up saving me from starting to drink again. I fell in love with JHope for some reason he just resonated with me, and he became my bias, and my bias wreckers are Jimin and Suga.

Seokjin...Hoseok

I started buying box sets, photo cards, stickers anything I could find. Me and my daughter bonded over BTS, we watched videos together and watched the muster together. We both got up early in the morning and watched it and loved it.

I got a global membership, joined a few groups for ARMY over 40 and made a lot of new friends who don't think I am weird for loving a group of younger men and they are men... My husband calls them that Boy Band from Korea, I told him they are men and he better watch it or I may just head over to Seoul to take care of them.

That is the story of how I became an "Older ARMY" and I am an ARMY for life.

To BTS, thank you for saving me when I didn't realize that I needed saving. RM, Jin, Suga JHope, Jimin, V and Jungkook, I purple you!!! You taught me how to love myself.

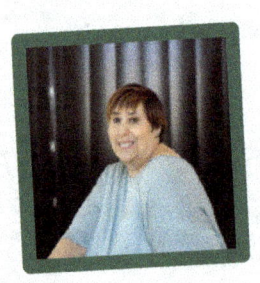

Gail

Jimin...Jungkook

BTS is Part of My Life Story

I am a single mom of 2 teens, 47 years young. I discovered BTS in 2019. Prior to this I was going through a bad break up from 2017 which became a health issue. So it was a lot to deal with. I actually stopped listening to any kind of music at that time. The saying is true when you are happy you enjoy the music but when you're sad you understand the lyrics. So, I just didn't want to be reminded of anything, so I just stopped listening to music altogether. I only listened to talk radio or podcasts. And if I did on the very rare occasion listen to anything it was old school R&B from my high school-university days which would bring me nostalgia and not any bad feelings or memories.

It wasn't until 2019. New Year's Eve. I decided to watch NYC NYE special in Times Square. BTS shows up and performs Boy With Luv & Make It Right. To say I was instantly intrigued is an understatement. As soon as it was over the next week or so I was watching everything on YouTube about them. Finding out their names and watching MVs to YouTube reactors. I watched "From Nobodies to Legends 2019" and I just cried. I still show that video today to anyone I can talk to about BTS.

I have read comments in their videos about how they have saved so many people. Young and Old. And I can be included in that story as well. Their impact on people is something I have never experienced before. I used to dismiss k-pop as

others do now. But entering the world of BTS, and falling down the rabbit hole, I would never go back. My regret is I didn't discover them sooner.

I also joined Twitter for BTS only and have met so many ARMY moms and Noonas. It's a whole new world. I have such respect for these now men. The things they stand for. The things they do for us. How they appreciate us, their life and this ride. They all know this ride is not going to last forever so they appreciate every moment. I have never been so touched by music and a group or artist in my 47 years. These group of men are special. I have the utmost respect and love for them. I will be ARMY for life. (Might even move to Korea to retire.) My life now is filled with BTS. My playlist in my car is all BTS. My kids know I love them. They make fun but they do not disrespect me and have even chosen their own bias'. I will never tire of them. In my eyes, they never gave up against all the hardships they endured; I will never give up on them.

I still get a lot of backlash and negative comments about loving BTS. Why is a grown-ass woman-mom pining over a "boy band group"? I used to try to explain and show and prove. Now I just say they make me happy. Period.

Juujeee7

My Galaxy of Eternal Happiness and Love

In 2018, it was during July when I was talking with my friends. Before I start I'll let you know that I'm in a girl's school. Few girls in my class were ARMYs back then and I would ask them, who is BTS and why they were so obsessed? Then they would make weird faces at me so I used to ignore it, but little did I know that soon I would fall for them. That day I started to have an interest in BTS, so I searched them on messenger, Facebook, YouTube and what not. In messenger I found a story bot suddenly which was for Suga mainly. So, when I started reading the story I was more attracted towards it and then I fell in love with Suga's personality. I thought why not know more about it? I went to YT and started searching about BTS. So, when I knew about them more I thought I would become an ARMY too. Sorry, I forgot to tell that I had a best friend that time and she became ARMY with me. I thought everything would go perfectly for me. I was a fan but wasn't an ARMY wholly. When it was November my final exams started and ended on December 10th. After they ended, I went for a vacation at my grandma's house.

In 2019, I had to prepare for my board exams in November. It was an important year for me. Also, another story before I go further, because this is where it all started, It was the reason I was so stressed and depressed. As I said, I had a bestie (well that's what I thought) but I was so damned wrong. She turned out to be a snake. When she needed contact with her BF she used me and when she was done, she left me and befriended another snake. During that time I was really hurting. I don't even remember the amount of nights and tears I spent crying. But that year I became stronger. I promised myself I wouldn't care or worry about those people who change their colours all the time. I was really stressed but still I was preparing for my exams and luckily my hard work paid off. In my 8th standard, I got A+ in all subjects. That's when I decided I didn't need any friends or a boyfriend or anyone. I'm enough for myself. So, I became more attached to BTS, and the songs were also helping me. That year was a painful one for me, but the best if I am honest.

And guess what? 2020 and 2021 were the luckiest and happiest years for me. Especially 2021. I felt like this year made me my "bestest" version, and even tho I was in depression sometimes, I didn't care. For me I found my eternal happiness, my galaxy, my love, my everything. If I say thank you to the boys, it'll never be enough because what they do is something so beautiful and amazing. The effort and hard work they put in everything they do is a heart and I'm thankful to my God a billion times for sending 7 angels to earth. They say no one is perfect but my BTS is perfect. RM, Jin, Suga, Hobi, Jimin, Tae, and JK, these 7 boys are most perfect because beauty isn't everything it's the heart that is important. And even writing this I feel like I'm not done yet. I have to write more. It's not describing them enough, not even 1%. Do you boys know why?

Because you are the best. You deserve everything in the world. Tell me it's happiness, love, care, attention, success, money, fans? EVERYTHING!! The way I found my galaxy, I found my stars, I found my happiness and I pray that you find it too. No one can love us the way you do, no one can make us laugh the way you do, no one else is crazy like you 7 and ARMYs. From my heart and everything I have, I pray to be a part of this craziness always. To be with Bangtan boys till the end because BTS and ARMY is together forever to infinity ∞. I can't look anywhere else. Forget about falling every day. I look at the 7 of you and I fall a trillion times. You inspired me to walk on my own path and do whatever I want. I want to keep working hard and not lose my confidence.

Now I became a stronger person in these 2 years. You guys helped me find my true happiness. And now I know what I want to become. I have stopped caring or listening to what people say. I'm not afraid anymore. I learned to always chase my dreams from RM, gained confidence from Jin, savageness from Suga, always to smile from Hobi, loving and cherishing others from Jimin, being myself from Tae, and giving my best in everything I do from JK. In short BTS HAS TAUGHT ME TO LOVE MYSELF AND SPEAK MYSELF, BE WHATEVER I WANT.

And now all I have to say is, BTS has given me so much more than I probably ever imagined. They loved me so much that I started loving myself even more. They found me and gave me shelter from a scary and unknown place. I want to tell you guys that now I'll do my best to love you and support you even if it means fighting the whole world. You're my togetherness forever to infinity. This will never end even when we die.

💜 BTS BOYS YOU ARE MY GALAXY AND I'M A STAR IN IT I'LL FOREVER BE WITH YOU, LOVE YOU, SUPPORT YOU WITH ALL MY HEART. YOU WERE WITH ME WHEN I NEEDED SOMEONE TO HOLD ME MOST. YOU ARE MY HOME AND MY DESTINATION and now I CAN'T STOP LOVING YOU.

Thank you so much for showing me what I was missing 🥺.

To my beautiful galaxy,　　　　BTS 💜 🪐
Lia Strike

Magic Shop

I officially joined army 23rd January 2021, and it was the best decisions ever. i hadn't listened to k-pop for a while, but bts made me fall back into it, and it's worth it. to be honest, i listened to bts' songs since 2015 (i was 8 years old). the reason why i became an army is because i was at my lowest and so tired of everything, even my family. to be honest i was about to suicide. i even wrote suicidal notes to my parents. but yeah I'm still alive and bts is the reason. i don't know how but suddenly magic shop was on my YouTube, and i listened to it. i cried a lot that day. i listened to it over and over again, and i decided not to suicide, but still i wanted to hurt myself. i was stubborn, but your lyrics kept playing in my mind so i didn't do it. and i started to be one of your fans. bts saved my life when nobody knew i needed saving. they comforted me with their songs. I'm always proud to be an army. 💜 i will stay with you guys for the long run. thank you for making my hard time easier. everyone told me to love myself, but you guys showed me how to love myself. please be happy always and be safe also stay healthy. i think that's all i need to say. (sorry for bad grammar :)
borahae 🧡
kimnuhaaa

Finding Strength in Broken Wings

"I BELIEVE IN MYSELF; MY BACK HURTS IN ORDER TO LET MY WINGS SPROUT."
BTS Wings

Believing in myself was something I struggled to achieve, it was an elusive idea and seemed extremely out of reach. Living had become an arduous task and at times I could not catch my breath. I am an English teacher, and I would arrive at school, enter my classroom and cry. I was filled with fear and anxiety, essentially I was lost. This incredibly low point in my life was when I accidentally found BTS, well it wasn't accidental, everything happens for a reason; right?!

Every day for weeks one of my students would put videos of BTS on my overhead projector and listen and dance. Most of the time I would barely be engaged, but today was different. The overwhelming feelings of insecurity, weakness, sadness, and depression were beginning to become all consuming. I could barely focus and then, "Spread, spread, spread my wings", the lyrics from their song, Wings, continuously played in the background. I stopped to listen and noticed, these lyrics were uplifting, exciting, hopeful and moved me in a way I could not explain. I asked her to play the song again, actually, over and over again. I was memorized and this was my initial encounter with BTS and since then I have never looked back.

This began my journey, who were these young men, what was this song? I was ferocious with my research about them. I needed to understand why I was so affected by these simple lyrics and the seven young boys who were singing. I had thousands of questions. I went back in time to learn everything they did, how they started, about the struggles they faced, small meet and greets and the music, most of all the music. For the first time in a long time, I felt stronger.

As I discovered more about BTS, I became increasingly involved with their message, even though BTS are superstar performers and worldwide idols, they also experienced struggles, sadness and yet continuously express emotions of love and support to others. Their message gave me a sense of hope and a growing realization that with inner strength, I would regain my peace and happiness and foster a belief in myself. The unconditional love, mutual respect and understanding they possess as a group is remarkable. They are a family, and they treat us, A.R.M.Y., as a family too.

Becoming an A.R.M.Y. has allowed me to meet and connect with so many wonderful people, especially moms with like interests and struggles. We can relate to one another, and we all have a love for the boys, what I have encountered with this fandom, or should I say community, has empowered me to grow, encouraged me to be fearless and believed in me when I didn't believe in myself. Flying across the country, from Atlanta to Los Angeles for the Jingle Ball to see BTS and meet some wonderful ladies was no problem at all. Receiving their support, and understanding the messages from the boys themselves, through music, charity work and a general love for everyone, I am becoming a better version of myself. They gave me the strength, coupled with the camaraderie and the music to recognize that I can do anything, I could believe in myself. All I needed to do was "spread my wings."

The message BTS conveys to the world is universal, to love yourself and believe in yourself. The message BTS has given me is a promise; continue to move forward because you never walk alone. Everyone has struggles, insecurities and fear, life is rough and times such as these will engulf us, but we must continue to push towards our goals and continuously learn to love ourselves.

"Save Me, I'm Fine" is the anagram tattoo I have on my arm with one of the Love Yourself flowers connected, these words, so simple and complete, reminds me to be conscious of my thoughts, feelings and to always love myself, they give me hope, and strength to acknowledge sometimes I might need saving, however ultimately with BTS, I'm Fine.

    Jodie DeGruy-Fowler

Spring Day

I'm Fine

I Need You

Save Me

Best of Me

ZERO O'CLOCK

Euphoria

Promise

Make It Right

Magic Box

Life Goes On

The Morning Will Come Again

Hi!

My name is Shambhavi. I'm 17 and from India.

Before telling about my dreams, I really want to thank BTS and especially Kim Namjoon for changing my perspective towards life.

I came to know about kpop back in 2012 when the legendary song "Gangnam Style" was traveling around the world. That's when kpop gained my interest and a year later I was all over the new BigHit boy-band that debuted.

Ever since I was a child of 4 or 5, my parents always told me how brilliant and sharp minded I am. They have been so happy about how confident I am on stage and what a strong stage presence I have. I'm glad about my god gifted talent. Who knew that this love for stage is only going to increase day by day to a point that all I wanna become is a performer and entertain the world... But as we all know that life is not all colors and Rainbows, it's stone and pebbles for the majority. I was no exception. Every Asian would relate with me when I say that I was forced to stop thinking about my music career as it won't lead me anywhere (brown parent problems, uff) But me being me, how can I just leave my only source of happiness? In my case it was music, more specifically BTS. The once gloomy child started smiling, the once anti-social kid started talking, the lad that once started believing the dreams are nothing and it's just fairy tale started believing that dreams can come true as well. You can

Achieve something which might seem impossible if you have the courage. All the 7 guys whom I've grown so fond of, literally showed me a different part of life. A part I never knew existed.

I'm in my last year of high school and hopefully would be in South Korea next year... Why? To pursue my dreams as an artist or maybe a lyricist. Some compromises and sacrifices have been made, many tears shed... But as "someone" has rightly said, "After every harsh winter, we will come across the beautiful spring".

I wholeheartedly thank those 7 boys who changed my life for good. I can never not have enough words to thank them.

A small thank you to Kim Namjoon for making me more mature. Thanks to Kim Seokjin for making me more confident in my skin. Thanks to Min Yoongi for making me learn how important hard work is. Thanks to Jung Hoseok for making me learn that being happy and positive can make you overcome the biggest challenges. Thanks to Park Jimin for making me realize the worth of every small thing. Thanks to Kim Taehyung for making me learn that being myself is better than being someone who wants to be accepted by everyone. Thanks to Jeon Jungkook for making me realize that doing our best is very important.

Thank you BTS for everything. You might never know me but it's a promise to you and myself that I will for sure make y'all proud.

Happiness

At first, I didn't know much about the outside world. I only knew some of the American singers such as Justin Bieber or Taylor Swift.

One day in school, I heard the Fan Chant. I was stuck on the names and wondered about the people, but my curiosity only lasted for a few hours.

One day, my best friend suggested that I watch Korean dramas. I didn't want to at first, but she forced me and said that I will like it. As she said, I really liked them.

Once an ad popped up, it was a music video. The name of the MV was 'Magic Shop'. The song nearly made me cry and healed me at the same time. While listening to it, I didn't know the meaning. It was after that I searched for it. But at that very moment I felt the song with my heart.

Even before knowing the meaning, the song touched my heart. Every night I used to cry with my pillow but now I listen to 'Magic Shop' and smile.

Like everyone says, first you listen to the music, search for their names, see some more funny videos like RUN BTS and then you are inside a room which you cannot escape.

I may not promise to have been here from the start, but I stay till the end. By end, I mean the day I die. Your music plays a very important role in my life. It is like chocolate to me. Smooth and sweet.

— Garima

My Journey to the Purple Land

My name is Emmaculate Baloyi, and I am 20 years old. I live in South Africa (Pretoria). Currently I'm on a gap year. My dream is to be an accountant. I love taking pictures, cooking, traveling, and singing even though I am a bad singer. I am an introvert. I love spending time alone and lately I love sleeping a lot. I discovered BTS around April this year. My journey to the purple land started when I saw a video of BTS singing, boy with luv, on TikTok and I fell in love with that song immediately. I started to watch their MV on YouTube and I fell in love with everything they do. As a "baby army" I'm still learning more about BTS. My journey to the purple land is exciting, adventurous, and full of joy. I am so proud to be part of ARMY, ARMYs are the most wonderful people I've ever met. I enjoy watching run BTS a lot. BTS's songs makes me happy, and I just can't wait to go to their concert. I love BTS with all my heart. I wish to be as intelligent as RM, I wish to be a great dancer like Jhope. He moves his body so freely, I wish to be cool as JungKook I'm in love with Taehyung's voice. I wish to be confident as Jin. With Jin's confidence I can achieve anything in life. I wish to be cute and humble like Jimin and I also wish to play a guitar, and drums like Yoongi. I fell in love with basketball because of Yoongi. Since I started to stan BTS I've become happier and my skin is glowing. I'm so proud to be part of making history, topping charts, collecting awards and making history with BTS.

hello

The Story Of A Girl Who Found Her Greatest Blessing

I am not good at telling stories but telling about how I found my way to BTS is a story I'll never get tired to tell. Shall we start?

Once upon a time, in a world that most people are in quarantine because of a pandemic, a girl named, Vea, saw a lyric video of EIGHT by IU feat. SUGA of BTS. She listened to the song and was amazed by the rap part. She became curious. Who is this guy named SUGA? She knew about BTS because they are really popular in her country, but she doesn't really know who they are, individually. Then, she started to search them on the internet. Little did she know, it will be the start of her most beautiful moments in life.

The first video that she stumbled upon was the Carpool Karaoke with James Corden. It was such a fun to watch. After that she started to watch other compilation videos and started to listen to their music.

The first song she listened was "Spring Day" because she remembered that one of her friends told her to watch its MV; that it was a really heart-touching song. So, she did. And it was indeed a beautiful song. Thanks to translations of the lyrics and beautiful MV, it made her heart melt.

Listening to their music made her fall in love so deeply. As days goes by, she started to realized why ARMYs around the world love these seven men so much! She fell in love with their music, passion, personalities, and love for each other and for their fans, ARMYs.

On May 9, 2020, a girl named, Vea, became an ARMY! BTS became her comfort and happiness in a world that seemed to stop. BTS became her motivation and inspiration. BTS became her seven reasons. She found another family in BTS and ARMY.

As BTS and ARMYs celebrate their 8 years of togetherness, Vea is so happy and grateful to be part of the beautiful universe of BTS and ARMY. It was more than a year since her curiosity led her to her greatest blessing. And she will walk with them even

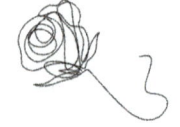

Until their journey as BTS ends. She will love them more than this life allow her to. She will choose them, every day and always.

She is me.

They say "curiosity kills" but for me it's the way I found my greatest blessing — BTS.

BTS songs are full of wonderful stories and messages and for us, ARMYs, BTS will always be part of our beautiful story.

Angels of my Life

Hello,

MY life just changed when i met BTS. They worked as The Angel for me which guides you to the right path. When I met them I realized that there is no gender in doing makeup, singing, or dancing. I discovered that I should be myself rather than changing myself for other people in the world. BTS taught me to love myself. They told me to focus on studies and respect the people who disrespected them. After all this, HOW CAN ANYONE HATE BTS? THEY TOLD ME TO RESPECT THE PEOPLE WHO DISRESPECTED THEM, EVERY TIME WE SEE THEM!

I am so lucky to be born in the Era where there are ANGELS LIKE BTS.

THERE ARE 7 BILLION IN THIS WORLD AND THERE ARE 7 MEMBERS IN BTS WHICH MEANS EACH MEMBER IS 1 IN 1 BILLION.

I LOVE BTS <3

보라해 방탄소년단
Leisha

A Journey of a lifetime:

I'm not so sure where to begin what I want to say, since so many emotions are coming towards me as I'm trying to tell my story. My story with BTS. Writing that sentence down warms my heart, knowing that I am part of something so special, the mesmerizing world of Bangtan Sonyeondan. 💜

I'm Virág (but you can call me Viri), a 19-year-old girl from Hungary (the centre of Europe), living in Budapest. I was only 14 when I first met BTS. I saw Dope playing on TV, and I was quite surprised by how catchy the song was. I immediately looked them up on YouTube, and that's when the miracle happened. I found many, many good songs of theirs and I started listening to them. I watched the translations of each of their songs, and I started following their lives. It was the best decision of my life. I became so close to them and since then, I have never left their side. I was there, even though I couldn't attend to any of their concerts due to my age, I was there. I listened to what they wanted to tell us through their songs, I watched them and supported them from my heart. Back then, no one around me knew

my story with BTS

about them, or even if they did, they laughed at them and at me as well for supporting them. I did not care about that, because the only important thing was for me to find happiness and joy, and I found it in BTS. I found everything I was looking for, and even things I didn't know I needed in my life. They helped me to get through difficulties in my life, and they taught me so many things. Hearing their stories made me think about my life, and how not to give up, even when things go wrong. I didn't love myself back then, I actually hated myself, the way I looked, my appearance, everything in me. They encouraged me to be brave, so I stood up for myself, and I managed to fight until I was satisfied with myself. Now I can bravely tell you that I love myself, and it's all thanks to BTS. During the pandemic, I faced so many difficulties, I lost family members, and I had to graduate after a year of online school, but they were there for me. I especially want to thank them for their song Life Goes On, which has a huge impact on me every time I listen to it. They gave me hope with that song, they lifted me up from the ground, and I'm truly thankful for that.

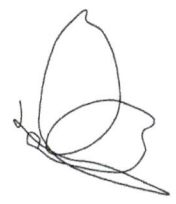

I couldn't imagine what was it like to love someone as much as I love BTS. I admire and adore each member equally. They are so unique, talented, and truly are amazing people. Their own, separate worlds, their personalities inspire me every day. I really look up to each of them.

I want to thank you Namjoon, Jin, Yoongi, Hobi, Jimin, Taehyung and Jungkook for working hard for your dear ARMY day by day, and for loving us unconditionally forever. You mean the world to us, just as much as we mean the world to you. This relationship between us is irreplaceable, unbreakable and is for a lifetime. I send you lots of warm hugs from Hungary, I really hope to see you as soon as possible, and remember: We are always there, we got your back no matter what.

Viri

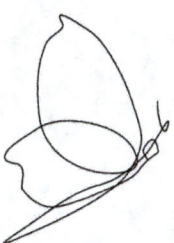

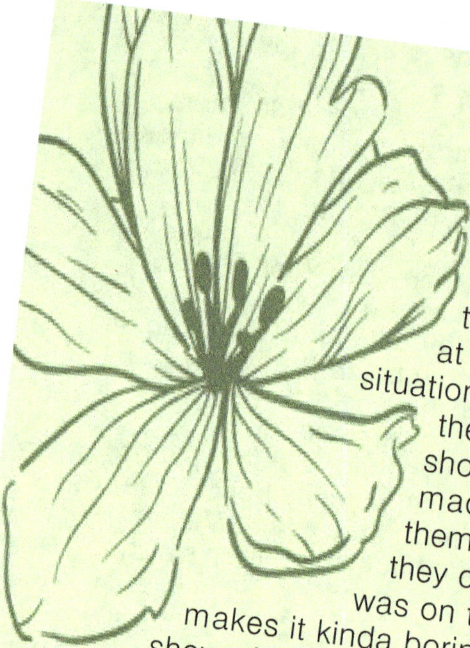

Love at the Right Track

Many BTS fans often say that BTS came in their lives when they are at the most difficult situation and that BTS gave them inspiration, showed them light and made them love themselves, but for me they came when my life was on the right track which makes it kinda boring already. They showed many colors to it that every time I hear their music I felt happy and proud that I stan the right group. They taught me how to dream big and do what I want to become happy. More than anything they made me realized that I chose the right person (my husband) who loves me with all my flaws and who would support me buying my merch 😆. Listening to their music gives me comfort.

Mooniea

Growing Up With BTS

Hello! My name is Cloudin, and I'm here to share my story of how I discovered BTS with you!

I discovered BTS in September of the year 2015. I was going through one of the most painful stages of my life, which I found out later on was how most ARMY came to know about BTS too.

I am from Egypt, but I had lived most of my life in Kuwait with my parents and younger sister. During August 2015, I had been waiting for my results from Cambridge and unfortunately, I had done very badly, barely passing in 2 very important subjects. Before that, I had lived my whole life being the "smart" student, so this for me was devastating and it meant that I could have possibly ruined everything that I had worked for because then I wouldn't be able to get into the good college that I wanted, which was Dental school. I remember I spent the whole day crying when I found out and decided to kind of punish myself by not going out or doing anything that I liked and to focus only on studying. I decided to work even harder. The very next day I had already started preparing for my re-sits (you can take the exam for the same subject again during another session to try to get a better grade in the Cambridge system) and one of the subjects I was retaking was Maths so on some days I'd listen to music while working on it.

Sometime during September, I had started becoming discouraged and couldn't continue studying anymore. Then one day, I was going through Facebook and came across a short video of BTS's performance of Let Me Know from the Red Bullet Tour. I was absolutely mesmerized by the song and Jimin's high note (Now let me, now let me, now let me iiiiiin) so I became a fan immediately!! I decided I'd look up the full song then I looked for more of their songs and came across songs like Dope and Boy In Luv.

This was not my first time discovering Kpop since I had friends who had told me about groups like Shinee, Big Bang, etc. and while I did enjoy some of their songs, I hadn't felt like I wanted to see or know more until I found BTS. I was very impressed by so many things like how synchronized they were while dancing and how they could actually sing and rap so well while dancing to such a hard choreography. After that, I decided to actually look more into the lyrics and find out what they actually were saying in their songs. Gosh, I'll never forget the feeling when I was watching the lyric video for the song Tomorrow, it was like a hit right in the face. How could a song in a language that I don't understand say exactly every single thing I felt and yet encourage me to go on and keep going?? Every single word felt like it was written for me, and I'll never forget the line that said, "It is darkest before the sun rises".

Since then, I started listening to their songs while practicing maths equations. Then later in November when HYYH Pt. 2 dropped, I got to enjoy songs like Butterfly and Baepsae which I could also relate to.

I had finished my re-sits in November, and I was only a few months away from high school graduation and at some point, I felt like I wasn't sure of who I am or who am I going to be or what will life be like beyond high school without my childhood friends, and there was still the fear of what if I didn't do well in my re-sits, what will I do then? I basically felt scared, and I just had so many questions. Butterfly resonated with me because of that.

Even Baepsae resonated with me because at that time

whenever I'd complain from something, I'd get responses like "Oh you have it easy now, back in my day we would have to do this and that" and how my generation is just "lazy" which is not true at all and was frustrating to me! It was just insane how BTS kept releasing songs that I could dance to and at the same time relate to. It only made me love them more.

Ever since then, it has felt like I have been growing up with BTS. With every comeback, it would somehow fit so well with my current situation in life (I was born in 1998 so I guess maybe I related so much cause I was going through similar stages as the boys?). The Young Forever album released right after my high school graduation, and I got accepted into the Dental school that I wanted to go to! Wings albums when I had just started college and was living on my own back in Egypt. You Never Walk Alone with Spring Day when I started facing some problems at college. Even going through the DNA phase when I had liked someone, then the Fake Love phase when I was going through another rough patch in my life because of the people surrounding me at college; I had changed into a version of me that didn't feel like me anymore and I hated it. Then came the Answer album and the Epiphany that I should love myself just as I am. After that, came MOTS Persona and MOTS 7 that I could also relate to in many of the songs like Intro: Persona, UGH, Inner Child, Zero O'clock and got to enjoy the other songs too and cry as an ARMY in We are Bulletproof: The Eternal. Then came the pandemic and Dynamite and BE which helped me survive what would have been a very dark time without BTS. And finally, Butter and Permission to Dance are how I got to end my final year of Dental school and graduate (currently still waiting for the results, it will probably be out by the time BTS hopefully get to see this)!

These past 6 years, I have really felt like I was growing up with BTS as if I'm a living part of their story. I am so thankful to God that he let these 7 boys be a part of my life. I really don't know how I would have survived all those things without them. Thank you BTS for everything! I love you and I hope my story will help remind you just how much positive impact you've had on many people in this world. Keep going and I'll always be cheering for you! Fighting!

              Cloudin

Delayed Reaction

I didn't like them at first. I thought they looked like thugs. I laugh to myself as I look around my very BTS inspired room. How they changed everything about me. From my language and mannerisms to even my choice in dog names.

I rediscovered them during the Wings era. A random YT search presented a video and I clicked to watch. When I saw Mr. Park Jimin in the center position in the opening lines of the song Blood, Sweat and Tears, it was over. Was this the same BTS as in No More Dream? Gone were the bad boy vibes and heavy eyeliner, and in its place were seven very sleek, sophisticated men with tight harmonies, delicious concepts and superior choreo.

I spent the next weeks devouring all I could on YT about them. I did internet searches about their personalities, favorite foods, habits, etc. My favorite early videos were of them sleeping. I thought they were precious, alluring, funny, enchanting, and very sexy.

And with my new eyes, their early work I appreciated with the fervor of a new fan. It all told a story, from the first day. The world of the BU enticed me. It took time, of course, to devour all the material, and not yet being on social media, the going was slow.

I didn't get on Insta or Twt until December 2018. I was afraid of other Armys. I was in my 40's. Would I be accepted? Would I be mocked? Insta was a first safe venue. Mostly pictures and a little talk here and there. Then, I jumped into the deep end. Twt.

A whole new world opened up for me. Even though I was a fan since 2016, I feel like winter 2018 was my real birth as an army. I remember I wouldn't barely admit that Jimin was cute when I first replied to an army's post. I know that the earliest armys I met are still with me now. Through BTS, I found a community of loving souls of all ages. We share the same heart. And there will always be drama on social media, but I have never been treated badly about my age, which is something I have always been sensitive about. I don't have my own family or any children. BTS and BTS Army has become my family. We have weathered happy times, sad times, hard times, births, deaths, Covid and they are my strength when I have none left.

So, my path in becoming an army happened very organically, starts and stops, and eventually they became my everything. I leave you with my favorite lyric. It hangs in my room, and I think it sums up what being an army really means to me.

"On days I hate being myself, days I want to disappear forever let's make a door in your heart. Open the door and this place will await. It's okay to believe, the Magic Shop will comfort you." - Magic Shop, BTS

Thank you for letting me share.

Kimberly, Pink haired Programmer, SoCal Army, Jimin Bias, OT7 always.

Losing Everything and Finding Love

How did I find BTS? Maybe they actually found me? It's almost like somehow they knew that I needed them, so much, in my life. My life as I had known it, fell apart. Through no fault of my own, I lost my marriage, home, possessions and my granddaughter. For a year and a half, I was homeless. I lived in a women's shelter and felt like my life, at 69, was over. Little did I know that I was going to find someone to help me, put the pieces of my broken heart back together.

I raised my granddaughter as my own, from the time she was seven months old and at 15, when I finally got out of the shelter, found somewhere to live and got her back with me, she gave me a wonderful gift, though at the time I wasn't too interested, or impressed. She introduced me to BTS! I had absolutely no interest in listening to some K Pop group that I couldn't understand. I knew they sang some RAP and that sure didn't appeal to me. She started me out listening to 'Butterfly' and 'House of Cards'. I still remember thinking that there was beauty in these songs, that I couldn't understand. These songs still are among my favorites. I also listen to RAP now, but only by J-Hope, Rap Monster and AgustD. I'm obsessed. Lol.

First, I fell for their voices. I was starting to get 'hooked on a feeling'. Lol. I couldn't tell those guys apart. I didn't understand one word of their songs, except an occasional word in English that was scattered in the lyrics. They wore make up and dyed their hair exotic colors. In the end, it didn't seem to matter. Their music spoke to my heart, my loneliness, and my pain. They brought me comfort. I found translations to the lyrics on YouTube, watched their unbelievable choreography and couldn't get enough of them. Three and a half years later, I still can't get enough of them.

I learned that their talent and handsome, good looks were only a part of their appeal. They actually seemed to care and relate to their fans. Their interest also, was the change in the world, that they wanted to be a part of. This gave them substance and value beyond their music. I realized that they weren't out for just the fame and money. They were out to make a difference. They wanted to comfort their fans and give them hope for the future. They've accomplished that and so much more. They've found people who were hurt, lonely, broken and rejected and made them feel a part of their world. They've shown their fans, who they lovingly, call ARMY, that they matter. BTS really love us. We matter to them. They've given us an example of how we should live. True ARMYS are caring, accepting, there for each other, the world and as well, for BTS. Within ARMY, I've found a family who supports me and accepts me. My age, weight, or life circumstances, doesn't matter to them. They love me because we all love BTS and BTS has taught us to LOVE OURSELVES. BTS is not a fad. They are substance and longevity. I'm here with them for the rest of my life and to support and respect them and their life goals and choices. "They were only 7 without us," Now we're all here together.

BTS, I'll never be able to thank you enough for what you've brought into my life. No matter what other things you accomplish in this world, you've given us, more than enough. You've helped heal, love and accept. You've shown us that the world is small and despite where we are from, or what language we speak, we are all the same. You've taught me that above all, to "Love Myself", and that's what it's all about.

Angelize

BTS, my parenting tip

I came to know BTS this year, 2021. At a time when we are all confined in our homes. I was scared of the virus. Scared of the vaccine. Scared of the future. Scared even of the outside air. I was particularly scared of showing my own fears too much because I have a little soul who draws strength from me. He is scared, too and worried about not going to school, not seeing his classmates, not playing outside. I searched for ways how to teach him how to be brave, how not to give up easily, how not to be overcome by fears. As a modern mom, I used the internet to find tips and hacks and being online too often, for too long, exposed me to a lot of content. One of them is the hottest video from the most popular band on the planet - dynamite. Such an easy song to hum along to. I was not too keen on the lyrics. I was just focused on the feel-good vibe of the beats. Before you know it, the next video plays and Mic drop is such a mood. A bounce up song. Fierce. Then came Anpanman. The word hero was all I understood at first and it felt like there's hope in this world. Before I know it, I was playing song after song on repeat. Dancing along. Memorizing their names. Eager to consume more information about to them. Run BTS. In the Soop. Bon Voyage. The purple ocean swallowed me whole! Then I thought of sharing this with my son., so we can bond over music and dance... Before that, I had to do some digging. I wanted to know if they are appropriate for kids. After all, my son is just 8. I chanced upon a video telling their story from the beginning. How they struggled. How they fought until the verge of breaking. How they never let their fears and hardships get the better of them. How they laughed their hearts out in the face of adversity. Wow! It was a teachable moment. It sums up how we should thread through life and instantly I wanted my son to learn from them. BBQ More important than their skills and talents, is their grit... and that's what got me hooked. I consent for my son to be influenced by them. They are not just a band. They are role models... and that's when I became an Army, an army mom.

Dreamgiver

Lost

In 2019 I lost my dad to cancer. He was diagnosed in February and gone in May so we barely had time to adjust to the fact that he was sick, let alone that we were going to lose him. Together with my mom he was the heart of our family; he was the one who moved us forward, who made us all laugh, who kept us together.

He was also a great musician; a guitar player and singer who brought music into the lives of everyone he knew. I grew up listening to him play almost every day. My dad and I listened to music together, we sang together, we performed together. Because of him music permeated every moment of my life.

When he died my life became silent. I didn't realize it for a long time, but I stopped listening to music. I stopped singing in the shower and humming to myself while I cooked dinner. Car rides were silent when I was by myself, and I censored any songs that reminded me of my dad when I was driving with other people. There was a giant space in my

heart where my dad and music had shared a home.

Then, in the Fall of 2020 I saw a commercial on tv with a catchy tune that I couldn't ignore. It sounded like something I might have listened to when I was a teenager in the 90's and over the moon for New Kids on the Block. Not quite the same style but something about it felt comfortable and safe.

That song was Dynamite by BTS.

That song filled my brain; I couldn't get it out of my head. Suddenly I had music in my life again. I found the video on YouTube and saw them for the first time. They were so happy and friendly, I felt like I was being welcomed into their world. I watched more videos. The music filled me up. The empty space started to get smaller.

At first I was a little (ok, very) embarrassed that I was becoming obsessed with a K-pop boy band. It felt like I was regressing into my teen years and that was somehow wrong.

But as the days and weeks went by I realized that I was genuinely happy in a way I hadn't been since my dad had died. I didn't know it at the time, but for all those months I had been feeling guilty about enjoying music without my dad. Somehow, BTS helped me let go of my guilt and find my connection with music again.

So, I stopped feeling ashamed and I embraced my newfound fandom. I joined ARMY and jumped into the rabbit hole. The last 8 months have been filled with music and comfort and a feeling of joy that I don't feel guilty about at all. And it's all thanks to a "K-pop boy band" that turned out to be so much more.

Ctmdunham

My Journey

In Dec 2017, I had a car accident that put me in the hospital for almost a year. I found BTS browsing through YouTube. I enjoyed their music during long physical therapy sessions. While in my bed I watched Run episodes and other videos. They made me laugh and their message helped me realize I was going to be ok and to look to the future that I almost didn't have. They have given me a renewed sense of self. I don't think they know how many people they have touched.

Dragonmaid49

A day may come when we lose, but it is NOT TODAY!

Hi, I am a 51-year-old mother of two, a 23-year-old son and 13 year old daughter. Both of them do not like K-pop; however, in May 2018, my son, Caleb, introduced me to K-pop as a joke. He knows I typically do not like pretty boy bands, but I used to love N-Sync for their dance moves. I guess he thought maybe I'd like Big Bang. I didn't. They were too much for me. Then, he showed me BTS's video, "Blood, Sweat, and Tears." Meh. They're cute and can dance really well, but they look snobby and serious. I don't like them. He gave up. Fast forward to September 2018, I heard that BTS was asked to speak at the United Nations assembly and introduce their "Love Yourself" campaign. It was primarily focused on youth. Even though, I was far from being a "youth", I recall struggling as a young person. I was abused as a child, so I hated my life back then and was so angry all the time. I never allowed myself to be happy, have fun, and enjoy life. Hated any pop music or cute things. I listened to RM's speech and was very impressed. I decided to give BTS a second chance. I searched on YouTube and found a video of BTS making fun of themselves. September 2018, after watching them act like absolute goofballs, I became an ARMY!

LOL! These guys are absolutely nuts, but, wow, are they cute and BOY can they dance!

After watching "Not Today," I identified with being "an underdog" and when they said, "there may be a time when we will lose, but it is not today!" The entire message of that song was what I needed to hear at that time. I was in the process of figuring out why I was losing my mobility and balance. Finally, after over 45 years and a genetic test, I found out I had an incurable, chronic disease and that I was going to lose my mobility (muscular dystrophy). I wanted to quit and let it get the best of me, but BTS said "not today!" Now, this has been my mantra! So many of BTS's songs have hit me right in the feels or strengthened me to the point of being ready to conquer the world. Then, you add their goofy, hilarious V-Lives and Run BTS!, it is absolutely impossible to be down. BTS has also taught me that it is ok to laugh at myself. When I even try to fret or cry, my ultimate bias, J-Hope, or BTS releases an album or song that gives me the energy I need. I am so thankful for BTS. They've made my life fun again. My husband and kids are very supportive of my BTS madness. Thankful for ARMY friends I've met from around the world as well. Being an ARMY has definitely changed my life for the better. Borahae!

WikiNui7

Zero O'Clock

Who do you turn to when you whole life is falling apart? Me, I turn to BTS. My mid-life "unraveling," as I call it (thanks, Brené Brown), gained momentum in 2018 after the first threads had begun to fray about four years earlier. Big life realizations and disappointments in 2018 led to feelings of sadness and loneliness settling in as if they had decided to be my best friends.

My already strained relationship with my parents was further strained, and I didn't have close friends, but I was married and had a teen son. I was far from alone, but lonelier than I'd ever been. That was the year my son got into BTS.

BTS did not introduce me to the Korean culture or language. My son, a Korean adoptee, did that. In order to best parent him, I had started learning the language and culture before he joined our family as a baby in 2006. Even as a baby he loved popular music, so K-pop had been a part of our family for more than a decade. An exchange student who had lived with us and returned to South Korea in 2013 was our first introduction to BTS, but it didn't click with my son then. It was five years later that something about the group clicked with him.

I had been following them casually for years; the first song I remember hearing was "War of Hormone." I knew when they appeared on US shows, but only after my son began to show me videos did I decide I needed to know their names. "Mom, you have to watch this video when RM tells Jimin he's got no jams. It's so funny." I knew RM, but which was one was Jimin. I needed to know. Initially it was a way to connect with my teen, who as happens during this stage of life, was growing more distant. But any BTS fan knows that learning their names is the first step toward joining the fandom.

There is a saying among ARMY that you find BTS when you need them most. This is certainly true for me. While the previous year had been hard, what was coming in 2019 was worse. I identify the Beatles-inspired performance on the Stephen Colbert show in May 2019 as my ARMY date. BTS World came out that summer and I began playing. Each time I opened the game it was like meeting up with my best friends, at that point truly my only friends.

In July, my relationship with my parents effectively ended. Watching old VLives and the Met Life concert, playing the game and listening to their music gave me strength and comfort to get through that final visit with my parents. As an only child, this was extremely difficult and it was something I had to process alone, since my spouse was not empathetic. For the next six weeks, my sadness deepened. Joy was found in BTS.

A trip to Korea to visit family and friends in September 2019 was a kind of reset, as I feel most at home in Korea. But the trip also highlighted growing issues in my marriage. In December, I told my husband I wasn't happy and while he agreed to make things better, nothing truly changed.

Through all of this, BTS was my emotional center. Their music comforted me, BTS World made me feel connected even if it was just an illusion, and their various other content made me laugh. I had started writing a novel inspired by BTS in May 2019, and by the end of the year, it was almost finished. My greatest moments of joy during this period of my life were related to BTS.

Then came 2020. It was, of course, a stressful year for everyone. For me, the stress of my marriage crumbling added to pandemic stress. As everything shut down and I was cut off from even the acquaintances in my life, while having to quarantine with my soon-to-be-ex-husband, an interesting thing happened. A woman who had been a casual friend, group texted me one day looping in another of her friends who was ARMY. My friend had seen a BTS video on YouTube and wanted to talk to ARMY about it, so she put us in the chat together because she knew that we would understand. This was the beginning of my first beautiful ARMY friendship. These two women and I began texting several times a day, mostly about BTS. But over time, our friendships deepened, and these women became a lifeline for me.

By the end of April my husband and I had decided to divorce. That same month I met my second ARMY friend in a Twitter ARMY group chat. We shared some life situations in addition to our love of BTS, and we became fast friends. Early on, we would talk for hours on the phone as we got to know each other. In May, I posted about my novel on Twitter and came to know my third ARMY friend. An avid reader, this woman fell in love with my characters, and our friendship grew from there.

I titled this "Zero O'Clock" because I feel that BTS helped me reset my life. This song is special to me because it reminded me during my darkest times that the sadness wouldn't last forever. After my first divorce hearing, I listened to it on repeat as I sat on my sofa and cried.

그래도 이 하루가 (But still, this day)

끝나잖아 (will end)

초침과 분침이 겹칠 때
(When the second hand and the minute hand overlap,)

세상은 아주 잠깐 숨을 참아
(the world holds its breath for a very brief moment)

Zero O'Clock

And you gonna be happy
(translation credit: doolsetbangtan)

The song brought comfort; it gave me hope that this sorrow-filled stage of life would end and that I would find happiness again.

As I write this on Mother's Day 2021, I can say that I have found joy again. Not every day is happy but there is joy, and beauty, in every day. My three closest friends are the women mentioned above. Two do not live in the same state I do, yet they have supported and encouraged me through one of the hardest periods of my life. I have met both of them in person, and regularly spend time with the friend who lives in my city. Additionally, I have received so much love and support from ARMY on Twitter and have made many friends there that I hope to someday meet in person.

This submission was prompted by a post on Twitter today that said BTS makes me feel loved. Honestly, without these seven men whom I've never met, I wouldn't have love in my life right now. I am divorced and spending the year getting reacquainted with myself before I consider dating again. My teen son, of course, does love me but teen boys aren't known for their affection. I have no relationship with my parents or extended family. Most of the people I know in real life are more casual friends or acquaintances, no one who shares deep affection for me. Almost everyone has someone who is special to them and whom they are special to as well—parents, siblings, extended family, significant others, children. I have my son, ARMY friends and BTS.

Without BTS, I don't know if I would have had the courage to reclaim my life and rediscover what it means to love myself again. I'm certain that without BTS I would not be connected to the three friends, and countless other ARMY, who brighten my days. And, honestly, as ARMY I feel love from BTS themselves. I know that sounds ridiculous to those who haven't experienced it, but it's true.

One day in early March 2020, I was talking with a friend about BTS's Carpool Karaoke appearance. Another friend walked in and observed this conversation and asked, "Amy, what are you talking about?" I blushed a little, and responded, "BTS on Carpool Karaoke." My friend smiled and said, "I figured. You were so engaged; you look so happy when you talk about BTS."

It was a telling moment. It's hard not to be happy when you are talking about someone you love and are passionate about. I owe BTS so much. Because of them, I have more love and support in my life than I could have imagined 18 months ago. Thanks to them, I have accomplished my goal of publishing my novel and have the hope of publishing more.

I still have lonely days, but the deep sadness is gone. I hope to someday have the love of special person in my life, I'm but learning to be to be enough for myself. Overall, I'm happier now and I owe so much of that to BTS.

For me BTS=LOVE.

unsinkableamy

Lost Then Found

To show where I am now with BTS, I guess for me it's best to start what began my journey. In October 2018, I lost my best friend unexpectedly, in the form of my mom. This was the most painful thing I've been through since my dad died, so here I was just a grown woman who felt like an orphan. I didn't know how to deal with the pain I didn't know what to feel any more about anything, and if I DID feel it, I got it wrong. I felt lost and alone. I don't know how I found BTS, but I was on YouTube and they had been on Jimmy Fallon, so I thought, heck they're cute when I played it and I was mesmerized The joy, their smiles, it touched a nerve in my heart. So, I looked them up on YouTube, trying to find out who they were, where were they were from, what their names were, how to say their names properly... and their music, oh my gosh, their music just opened my heart. I felt like with their music I could cry, but not only could I cry, but I could be happy, and it felt weird to be happy because my mom was gone. But I know truly that she wouldn't want me to be sad. My world has changed, but it felt better before. I feel like BTS brought color back into my life and not only did they bring color, but they also brought ARMY into my life and with ARMY, they brought me a new family. After my mom died my sister and I stop talking, I don't know why and even trying to reconnect with her I just couldn't do it, and so I just felt even more alone. But then you bring ARMY into the picture, and they are my best friends. People I never knew I was missing until they were there. So, BTS helped me find my smile and helped me feel something again. But with that they brought a feeling of 'I want them to have the world', because they gave me back my world. How can I thank someone for that? It's something so priceless, but they did it. So, I love them with all my heart forever. I will forever support them and lift them up the way they've lifted up so many of us. It's like you've found this beautiful thing and you will do what you can to not only see them succeed, but to thrive as well. They've earned that kind of dedication. When they say you don't find BTS, BTS finds you, and they won't find you until you need them. I believe it's 100% true, I really do. I have no idea what my life would be like without them now, and without ARMY.

Beccaisme7177

They Saved Me

In 2020 covid happened and I really fell into a super dark place - my country and state were in lock-down for quite a while. We still had quite heavy restrictions going into early 2021, and by then I was really feeling so isolated and having some really dark moments.

I don't know how but I happened to be on Facebook and some clips of BTS performances came onto my feed, I had heard of them before but never bothered to pay any attention as I had no interest in KPOP.

My first ever experience with BTS was watching their MAMA black swan performance, I honestly teared up watching that performance. I had been a ballet dancer for 15 years, it was my dream, and I was good at it, but to pursue a career in it was difficult and tough - I gave it up because of pressure from myself, and parents - I am now in law school, which is still something I like, but its not the same.

I instantly fell in love with Jimin and his dancing in black swan, and I just continued to watch more performances (ON, mic drop, idol, dynamite) and was really drawn in by their dancing being a dancer myself.

It's so difficult to say this but I really think I found BTS at the right time for me, I was honestly having some really dark thoughts being in lockdown for so long, and BTS, their songs, their lyrics, their personalities, run BTS, all of their content was so uplifting. Even though I'm very late in becoming army in 2021, I wouldn't have it any other way.

They helped me fall in love with dance again after being so depressed that I stopped dancing, I attended a few dance classes again, and started teaching a few ballet classes whilst studying law at university. It sounds cliche but they are one of the few reasons I wanted to continue. I am crying whilst writing this because it is so difficult to reflect on that very dark period of time and how BTS and their music have brought me so much happiness.

hhryt

BTS, the heroes of my life

There was a time when I always said, I just want to disappear. I don't want to live anymore. I was so down. In school nobody talked to me, they used to always make fun of me when I talk or do anything. I didn't have friends... I was so lonely, I felt that I was alone in this world, and nobody felt about me. I always prayed to God to make me happier and give me friends. Then one day I opened YouTube as usual and there was my happiness waiting for me. In my watch list there was a strange video I never saw before, so I decided to open it and they were BTS!!! I don't know what really happened but when I saw that MV and it was the first time for me to see them, I felt something strange. People make fun of me when I say this, so I don't really tell anyone about it, but when I first saw them I felt as if I knew them a long time ago. I really felt that I knew them even though it was my first time seeing them. And there I started seeing BTS' videos "RUN BTS", "MVs" and all the other videos. They really changed my life. They became my friends, and I was like "Why would I need any friends if I have BTS with me?" Even the closest people to me didn't do what BTS did. I don't have any friends, but I don't care about having friends here because I have the most awesome friends in Korea -"BTS", who else do I need? I used to listen to "Magic Shop" a lot because I felt that that song was about exactly what I was feeling back then. "Magic Shop" and "Butterfly" really helped me overcome my hard days. Of course, all the songs helped me overcome a lot of difficulties, but these two helped me to overcome the sadness that I felt a lot of time ago. Nowadays I listen to 'Life Goes On" "Dynamite" and all the "BE" album, I love this album a lot. And now every time I feel down I just listen or watch BTS and after that, I feel refreshed, so I really thank God so much that he sent me those 7 boys to make me feel the life and live happy again!

I really wish to meet BTS one day and be able to thank them face to face, but if that doesn't happen, I really want them to know that there is a girl who recently moved to Canada, who was new to everything. A girl who was depressed and lonely. And now I wasn't that way anymore because they made her feel alive and smile again!

Thank you so much from the bottom of my heart. I thank you guys for changing my life and making it a more cheerful and happy life. I love you all so much and I will always be an ARMY! I'm so proud of myself that I became an ARMY. Thank you so much, guys. I purple you all :)

Forever we will be together! Borahae

Sumaia

The New Discovery

I am mum of two and a vivid k-drama fan but for some reason I have never listened to k-pop songs. I chanced upon BTS in January 2020 when the pandemic was taking off. I am a healthcare worker so the stress at work kept increasing after every shift. I was on Facebook one day when i saw a video of BTS about the hustle life of BTS in America. There was a prank video where the members were kidnapped. I thought it was a movie only to release - they were artists. I quickly googled them, and I was shocked to find out how big they were. I was skeptical but listened to 'boy in luv' which was my first BTS song. To be honest, I LOVED it, then started listening to other songs, ON, APANMAN, SPRING DAY, DYNAMITE, BUTTER, SUGA'S INTERLUDE, J-HOPE'S MIX TAPE, and the like. Since then, I have been addicted to their songs. During the pandemic, I always played their songs at work to cheer the environment. People didn't understand but you could feel the sense of relief while listening to their soothing voices. I am surprised how I have become a strong ARMY in a short period of time. I have never been a fan of any artist or celebrity. I only listened to their songs or watched their movies, then it ends there. But with BTS I can barely stay away from anything that involves them. I watch Run BTS every week and even watch those I missed before I became an ARMY. The members truly are an inspiration to the youth.. I love all the BTS members, but my bias is J-hope.

Robbyneils

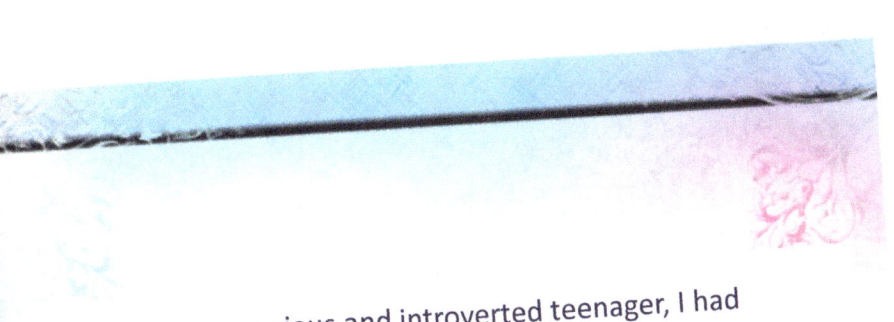

Being an anxious and introverted teenager, I had always underestimated my potential and seldom ventured out of my comfort zone. It was easy for me to make friends but never let them see the real me. This changed a couple of years ago when a friend introduced me to BTS's songs. Their songs are extremely emotional and meaningful. I got curious about them and started watching more of their videos. BTS's songs made me realize the importance of being confident in my abilities and stepping out of my bubble. In the song "Love Yourself", BTS emphasizes trusting and loving oneself "when in a maze". The lyrics inspired me to reflect on my personality and abilities. They helped me accept myself, understand my flaws and strengths, and encouraged me to build on them for

My Happiness

personal growth. I tried to be more open which resulted in me having really close friends. Last year as COVID-19 emerged I got into a fight with one of my best friends resulting in me breaking down. I didn't know who to talk too but BTS came to the rescue. Their songs make me smile and forget everything else. I also joined Twitter where I got to meet really amazing ARMY friends. BTS helped me get through hard times and become my supporter. They inspired me to learn new things. I started learning Korean and explored Korean culture. I don't regret falling in love with BTS for even a second. Fangirling them was the best decision I have ever made.

Bhuvi Mangla

김태형 미스터리

안녕 형 나는 bts에 대한 15
년 된 팬걸이고 처음 본 이후로 나는이 신비한
질문을 느꼈다 :
그의 얼굴에서 손가락과 손에 너무 완벽하고 저항
할 수없는.
나는 그가 이것을 알고 있는지 여부를 확인하고
싶습니다 ....
당신이 당신이 그런 아름다운 영혼과 귀엽고 무고한
사람이 라는 것을 알고 아래로 느낄 때이 태는 당신
이 최고뿐만 아니라 다른 bts
회원 알고하시기 바랍니다 하지 마십시오 나는 항상
당신을 사랑으로 당신을 지원할 것입니다....:)

DANA SHREE @ INDIA

Kim Tae-hyung Mystery

Hi brother. I'm a 15-year-old fan girl of BTS and I've had this question about this mysterious man since I first saw him: why are all of his body parts so perfect and irresistible from his fingers and hands to his face? I want to make sure he knows this........... Tae, I want you to know that you are such a beautiful soul and a cute, innocent person. Please know that you are the best, as well as the other members of BTS, too. I will always support you with love... :)

YOU'RE MY WORST KEPT SECRET

I am a busy working mum of 2. I had never been a fan of any artist before. My obsessions when I was a teenager were male and female athletes from quite obscure sports. And then my life got too busy to actually have a time-consuming hobby. Higher education, a PhD abroad, a first baby, a first job, then a house, a second baby... Music was always an afterthought, a few songs on a playlist on repeat, mostly "dad rock" songs, and that was it.

Because I had no time to actually sit down and watch movies or TV shows anymore, YouTube became one of my few pockets of escapism. I spent meaningless hours watching influencers or talk show snippets. This is how, sometime in 2018, I stumbled upon clips of a boy band from Korea performing "I'm fine" and "Idol" on the Jimmy Fallon show. I clearly remember loving the outfits, the choreography and obvious professionalism of those boys, even though I could not understand why everyone was deciphering every little detail

in the voice or moves of each member in the comments section. I simply thought, "I'm too old for this", and moved on.

Fast forward August 31st, 2019. I watched Safiya Nygard's video entitled "I got a kpop makeover". She used a lot of clips of music videos and explained how fashion-forward the industry was, and how by the end of her research for this video she had become quite the kpop stan. I suddenly remembered those boys from 2018 and typed "BTS music video" in the search bar. Blood Sweat and Tears was the first result. I started watching it and paused it after a few seconds and made the decision that changes every single army's life: "I JUST WANT TO KNOW THEIR NAMES." YouTube has several very good introduction videos on the topic. The rest is obviously history. Like everyone else, I fell down the rabbit hole to try to learn about and understand more than 6 years of content. The

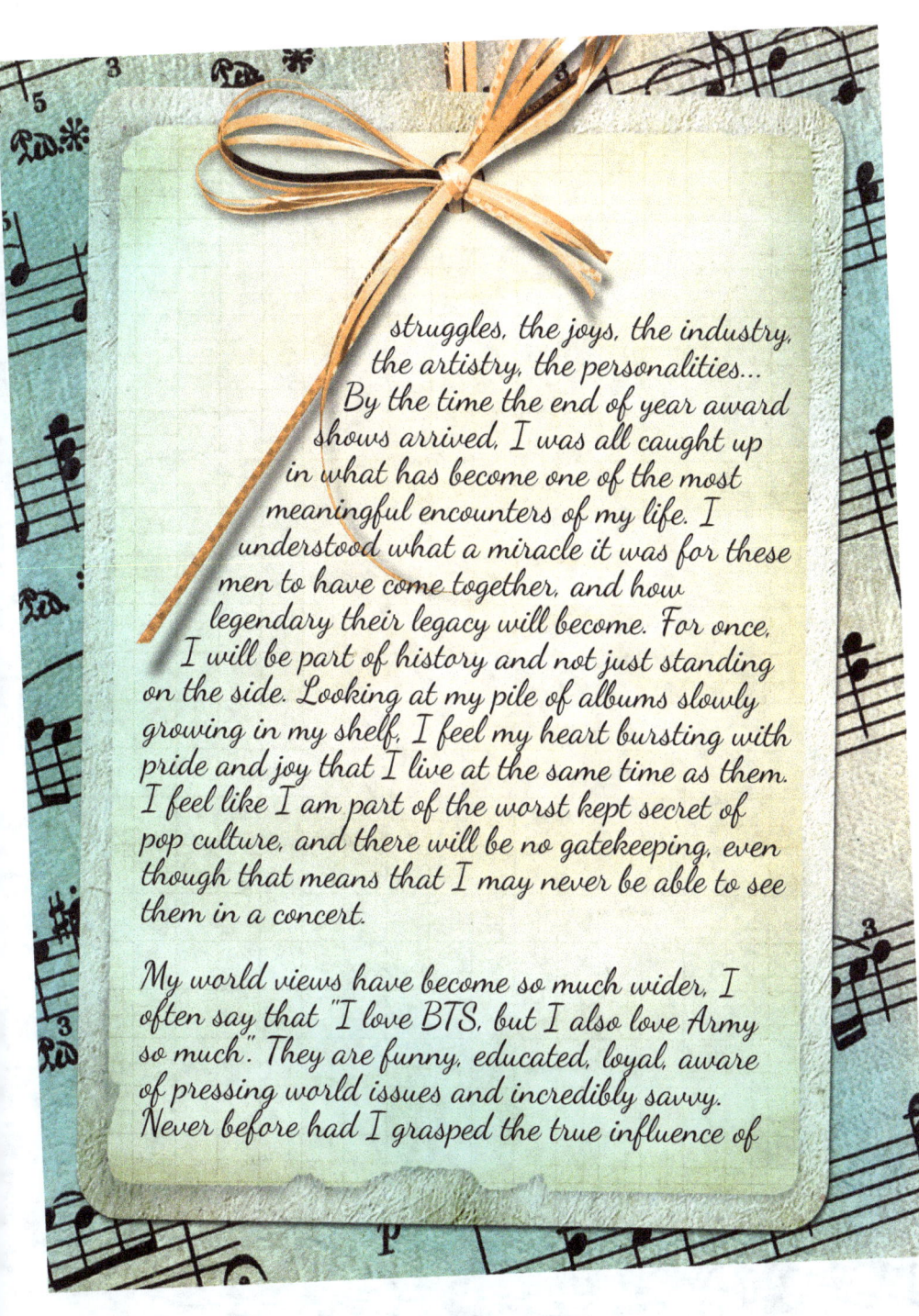

struggles, the joys, the industry, the artistry, the personalities... By the time the end of year award shows arrived, I was all caught up in what has become one of the most meaningful encounters of my life. I understood what a miracle it was for these men to have come together, and how legendary their legacy will become. For once, I will be part of history and not just standing on the side. Looking at my pile of albums slowly growing in my shelf, I feel my heart bursting with pride and joy that I live at the same time as them. I feel like I am part of the worst kept secret of pop culture, and there will be no gatekeeping, even though that means that I may never be able to see them in a concert.

My world views have become so much wider. I often say that "I love BTS, but I also love Army so much". They are funny, educated, loyal, aware of pressing world issues and incredibly savvy. Never before had I grasped the true influence of

soft power. As I am coming towards the end of my second year as an army, I reflect on the tangible influence they have had on my life: I am no longer overweight after more than a decade of struggles, I am in the process of a radical job change because I have finally grasped my professional value, and I have found a place in the world that is no longer just a wife, mother or employee: I am part of the most powerful army in the world, and I have made it my mission to be a listener and carer for anyone in this fandom who needs a hand or an ear.

The other day, my 3-year-old was in the car behind me after a long and tiring day, and she asked to listen to BTS. I put on their recent "Fix you" cover and after a few seconds she said: "mum, this song is making me feel better". Enough said.

Popfrench

BTS Gave Me Back My Smile

I'm not diagnosed with any mental illness, but I've been stressed and hurt by people around me which make me sad and depressed. Even the very person close to me is giving me a hard time. This has made me really sad. It makes me cry all the time and the smile has left me.

I'm blessed that I have four sisters and friends whom I talk to but it wasn't enough. I still feel empty, alone, and sad. Work and home are my struggles till this day. My sister who is a BTS ARMY introduced BTS to me when she was about to watch their Paris concert in October 2018. I have never heard of them nor of Kpop before. The first time I saw them was at the American Music Awards in October 2018 before my sister introduced them, their videos and music to me. The one who caught my attention was Taehyung. But since I was in a very dark place, I hadn't fully grasped them yet. So I didn't pay much attention until my sister talked to me about them. The first video I saw was their history of how they started, their

struggles and difficulties which immediately captured my heart. I felt their honesty and determination in the videos. Next was the House of Army which made me laugh for the first time. I quickly learned their names and talents. Then I watched their music videos and looked at the lyrics of the songs which touched my heart. I related to the messages of their songs, and they helped me cope with my sadness and struggles. Their videos make me smile and laugh. They were pure joy. My sisters saw the change in me...that I'm blooming. I admit that I was happy. They make me happy. BTS make me forget all the things that make me sad while watching them. They are very attractive young men and are extremely talented.

I joined the BTS ARMY fandom and met good friends. And that's when I fell deeply into the rabbit hole in just a few days. For me, what has been most important is that BTS is my comfort and happy pill. I am not embarrassed to be a fan girl. BTS has shown me what

some of us don't have which are a sense of closeness and amazing friendship. My world has never changed. I'm still in a place where I struggle at work and at home. I still don't know what to do but I have the 7 amazing young men who give me comfort and make me smile. They are my happy pill during my desolate lows. Especially late in 2018 when my dad was diagnosed with Cancer and after 6 months he passed away. BTS was there to comfort me when no one can. My sisters and I live in different countries, so I focused myself on what makes me happy. And that's BTS... they give messages like they are talking to me at the right time when I needed it. To me, RM, JIN, SUGA, JHOPE, JIMIN, V, & JUNGKOOK are a blessing in disguise. They may be young, but they are smart, talented, and full of wisdom. I will never forget what Suga said, "Take your hands off of what you can't control and get your hands on what you can change. As you and I continue in life, we will find ourselves in many situations out of our grasp. The only

"I'm not in a dark place anymore."

thing we can control is ourselves. Get your hands on the changes you can make because your possibilities are limitless." Now, although I'm still walking on thorns, I'm not in the dark place anymore because BTS gave me back the smile that I once lost.

Maria_V_tae

A Family Affair

Summer 2018: "She's a bit old to start fangirling", I thought to myself, when my 18-year-old daughter began gushing about a Korean boy band. But since she rarely shared things dear to her heart, I happily listened, but without giving it further thought. (Months later I was surprised to discover that a song I grabbed from her Spotify playlist was in fact "Change" by Whale ft. RM.)

"Would you like to watch their latest MV?" she asked sometime later. It was "Idol", and I have to admit, it was overkill for me, optically, as well as musically, and I was like "Ooooooookayyyy... not quite the music I'd choose for myself." However, the next video she shared was "Spring Day", and that was something else! I loved the track from the very first moment, and I was extremely intrigued.

That same summer, she explained that BTS were invited to the United Nations to give a speech. I was tremendously impressed by Namjoon, his words, and by the way he and the boys presented themselves. I still wasn't quite sure why they were chosen to address the UN but awe-struck on multiple levels, and by and by their music found its way into my playlists: "The Truth Untold", "Epiphany", "2! 3!", "Mic Drop"...

Fast forward February 2019: The Love Yourself, Speak Yourself Tour was announced, and my girl, who already had missed their Berlin concert 2018, was determined to watch one of the Paris shows. However, as a student, she was always short of money, and needed her parents to assist. As it happens, I love the city of Paris, so my only thought was: "When she's going, I will, too!" And since I was paying for the trip, she was fine with that. "So will you join me for the concert, too?" she inquired, and without a moment's hesitation, I said yes. These guys are nice to look at and make amazing music — so why wouldn't I go? But she added, "If you're really attending, you have to know who's who and a lot more!" So, she made me learn their names, get to know their discography, and watch their content. That's when I started slipping over the edge. I will never forget the day they performed "Make it Right" at Colbert's Late Show. They were sitting still, so I could practice their names. And I finally discovered which one of them was able to give me chills by the little growls in his voice.

Paris, 06-08-2019: It was the first time in ages that I'd been to a concert, and I was thunderstruck by their performances, stage presence, and by the mere atmosphere of a BTS concert. they reached out for me then, and I've never let go. However, it wasn't until fall that I would dare call myself Army. I remember watching a stream of the final Seoul concert, and crying like I never had before, because music never had affected me like that. They are able to touch something deep inside of me, something I had kept closed for the better part of my life — the part, where my feelings live, where everything is weak and raw and easily hurt — the part, I had stored away, because that was what I had learned as a kid: "Don't show others that you're weak. Don't give them a chance to hurt you. Don't cry over meaningless stuff."

I'm so thankful that BTS was finally able to crack open that shell! I'm still struggling with my feelings, and afraid to show my weaknesses, but it's getting better. BTS and Army are by my side, I'm on my way to accept myself, and maybe even one day, to love myself. I will forever be grateful for

- their music
- the joy they spread
- the inspiring thoughts they plant in my head
- the wonderful people I met thanks to them
- intensifying the bond between my beloved daughter and me

Still Paris

Happy Place

I love Emma Stone. I think she's a wonderful actress, funny and cute with great comedic timing. I'm also a big fan of SNL, having watched it pretty consistently since the Not Ready for Primetime Players in the 70's. I tuned into SNL on April 13, 2019, to watch Emma host for the fourth time, completely unaware my life was about to change. I don't recall any of the skits. I'd heard of BTS but wasn't at all familiar with them. Boy With Luv. How many of them are there?! How do they sing while dancing?! How do they keep smiling while singing and dancing?! What is the name of the tall blond guy?! What is the name of the smiling skinny dancer my eyes are drawn to?! MIC Drop. This song is so very different than the last one performed. The versatility that the song styles can be so dramatically different?! The skinny dancer again. The MIC MIC bungee guy in the blue-green shirt with the little vest-y accessory thing. The one wearing the Dorothy shirt, untucked on one side. Luckily I recorded the episode on my DVR. Is it possible to wear out a DVR episode because over the next two days I was in constant replay mode.

I texted a friend who's been ARMY since at least 2015 and said, "I now understand." I vaguely recalled a conversation we'd had about 2 years earlier when she explained their pop and rap styles. I laughed it off at the time. She asked who my bias was, then had to explain what that meant. My bias was Namjoon for a few days, then j-Hope (the smiling skinny dancer), and a week after that it switched again to Jungkook and remains so to this day. After our text convo, I remembered that the friend had posted a story on Facebook a couple years earlier about meeting a kpop idol while living in Osaka. Mad dash into her postings. The holy grail. She met j-Hope. Shook his hand. Actually, touched him. Talked to him. He talked to her. Every time I see her, I ask her to repeat the story from beginning to end. It's an adrenaline rush for both of us. A few weeks after the SNL performance, my daughter gave me the Map of the Soul: Persona CD as a Mother's Day gift. Inside, there's a poster. I learned their names and began to differentiate their voices in the songs. I took the poster to work and taped it to a wall. One of my coworkers told me she's ARMY and that she's seen them in concert. I discovered what ARMY means both as an acronym and as a concept. We started sharing photos and she recommended videos and older songs and albums. I've been a manager in healthcare administration for over 20 years and now it's a well-known fact within my organization that I'm a fan. My CEO encouraged me to bring in more posters and asked me for song recommendations. More than once, the CEO has asked me in a staff meeting of 100 people, "What's new with BTS?" I haven't blushed in years but find myself doing it fairly often.

By mid-May 2019, I realize I'm a baby ARMY and that I'm not just a fan but that I'm on a journey. I realize I've never had this strong of a connection with another group or singer. Sure, I've listened to other artist's music on repeat for a month or two, but then move on to something or someone new. As I approach my 2-year ARMYversary next week, I realize that in those two years I've listened to little other than that group on SNL.

My first opportunity to see them perform in person was at Jingle Ball in LA in December 2019. My daughter and I flew there that day, I was a nervous wreck until we stepped onto the grounds of The Forum two hours before the concert start time. The audience vibe was electric. They performed first. Three songs, 15 minutes total. MIC Drop. Make it Right, Boy With Luv (with Halsey!). The best 15 minutes of my life. Incredible.

I've been working from home for the past 13

months and all of the posters and photos from my office have been relocated to my home office, with many new additions to the collection. It's my happy place.

I've met wonderful, supportive people on social media, all sharing that same love. I often think of the influence these seven people have had on me personally, either through their music and lyrics, their playful interactions with each other, their emotional intelligence, and their respect and kindness. I often wonder how these seven people remain steadfast in their beliefs yet are also ever evolving. I often wonder how they remain so genuine, so authentic, so thoughtful, and so true to themselves while also being so famous. Jungkook recently commented in an interview something to the effect of, we're just regular guys. Agree to disagree as they are so unique and special.

They often express their concern for ARMY's health and well-being and health. I think about their health and well-being daily. I wish them to be happy, to live without feeling encumbered, to have small moments and to enjoy those moments to the fullest, to feel the strength that they provide to us to be returned to them a thousandfold, to love and to be loved.

How has my life changed since April 13, 2019? The world has changed dramatically in the past year, and although my family and friends have provided me with personal support, the most significant influence on my overall mental health and what has kept me in my happy place has been Kim Namjoon, Kim Seokjin, Min Yoongi, Jung Hoseok, Park Jimin, Kim Taehyung, Jeon Jungkook. BTS.

Annasanchez2x

How BTS Found Me

My life could be its own book or a Lifetime Channel movie. Things started out well, parents divorced when I was ten & we moved in with my grandparents. The years living with my grandparents were pretty great, but after my grandmother died, my mother moved us to Florida and my life became a sad drama. I ended up marrying the wrong guy for the wrong reasons and it ended in divorce. I've been single for the past 17 years. A little over 3 years ago, I had been following another kpop group but heard BTS was going to be on the AMAs, so I watched it. And that, my friends, was when I fell headfirst into the rabbit hole. I had thought they were arrogant and brash, but after just trying to find out who was who, and which one was the oldest, I discovered just how exceptional each member truly is. Their performance grabbed my attention, but their hearts and souls have kept me here and made me part of their ARMY. Their message of "Love Yourself" really helped me begin to accept myself and to realize I'm the one I should love. I get so much wisdom and positivity from these 7 young men from South Korea. They came into my life when, though I had my faith in God & knew He loved me and was by my side, I was feeling worthless and alone here on earth. Now I have 7 young men on the other side of this planet who tell me they miss me & that I matter and, though I'm terrible at it, I'm starting to make new friends in this ridiculously huge family called ARMY. 💜

skorealove_us

Growth: Discovering BTS, &; Myself

MY BTS JOURNEY

I stumbled upon BTS either very late 2016 or very early 2017 - I'll be honest it's all a bit fuzzy now, and I keep my YouTube history turned off, so the details of my first exposure will remain a mystery. I do remember the circumstances though, and like many other soon-to-be ARMY, I quickly fell down the rabbit-hole.

It all started by searching for some instrumental music to use for a D&D campaign I was running at the time (the Curse Of Strahd module for any fellow players). I was looking primarily for string-heavy stuff because a gothic horror, vampire-centric atmosphere needs strings! Anyway, I got very side-tracked as I often do, and started listening to violin covers - because who doesn't love a good violin cover? Eventually, I came across JuNCurryAhn's channel, which among other things, has many BTS covers. I had not heard of BTS, but I did like the covers and was intrigued - so I looked for music videos, and the rest is history.

At this time in my life, I was mostly listening to alt-rock, indie, some electronica, and some J-rock. I like listening to music a lot when I work because it helps me focus. I put relatively equal importance on lyrics and sonic appeal. I tend to dig through an artist's entire catalogue for things I like, but don't typically get invested in the artists themselves. I'm sometimes disappointed by what I find when I really look into them, and it can sour my appreciation for the music. So, I listen to a lot of different music, and like a lot of artists, but only respect a select few as people. I'm able to appreciate something much more when I can stand behind who made it and why.

Ok back to the story! So, it was somewhere between

2-4am in the pre-dawn hours of a cold winter morning when I saw my first BTS music video. I so wish I could remember which one it was, but I binged for a while, so I can't say for certain. I distinctly remember RUN and DOPE - BS&T was the newest thing at the time. I also watched some videos from other groups in the recommended list but am not sure which ones anymore.

Over the next week or so, I began my dive into oblivion. I don't know when or how, but at some point in those first few days, I started exclusively digging into BTS. Maybe it was the sound of the music, maybe it was the thought-provoking lyrics, maybe it was the sincerity in their eyes, or the tangible bond between the members - but something pulled me in. I watched dance practices, Bangtan Bombs, guides on telling them apart, and more music videos. One day very early on, like maybe a week or two or three in my journey - there was a new video. This video is what would cement my respect and adoration for BTS - this video, is what made me want to be ARMY. The video, as I'm sure you've guessed, was 'Spring Day'.

It was the first time I commented on a BTS-related video - I said something like 'Every frame is a work of art.' At the time, before all the theory videos came out (and as an ignorant American), I didn't know about one of the major meanings behind the video - but I could still feel the sentiment. That is so incredibly powerful. It is something a lot of people notice - there is an insane level of skill but also sincerity and passion needed to make people feel your art even without fully understanding it. When I did eventually learn of the incident, my appreciation for the song and for BTS as people, only grew.

I remember watching the promo performances on music shows, as I dove into their discography and other content. I was very confused but incredibly amused when I found RUN BTS. During the Wings tour, I would eagerly look for blurry fan-cams after every performance. I needed that rush, the excitement of something new. At that time in my life, I was 24, out of college with a made-up degree from a defunct art school that got me nowhere (Bachelor of Fine Arts in Visual Communication). I had recently quit working as a deli clerk in a supermarket and went from spending my nights frying chicken, to spending my days desperately looking for something - anything in a related field, just so all the time and money I (and my parents) had spent on education wouldn't have been for nothing.

Competition for jobs was so heavy and the market was saturated with plenty of people just like me. Even my student ADDY award in photography was useless, and I was breaking. After lots of failed interviews for full-time positions, I had gotten an offer from a temp agency - unfortunately the hiring company kept pushing back my start date... for three months. I was not making any money. To top it all off, what little pride/confidence I had left was stretched so very thin.

My husband (then boyfriend) had graduated only a year ahead of me and was already the support team lead at a growing web/marketing firm. I hated that I was relying on his kindness for a place to live, and that I wasn't contributing nearly enough to be fair. He taught me more code, how to use a CMS and troubleshoot site issues so I had more skills for my resume. He even convinced his boss to throw some contract jobs my way every now and then.

NOTE this is not meant to shame anyone who is in a similar position or who needs help supporting themselves - I am fully aware of my brain's tendency toward unreasonably self-critical thought patterns. There are also a lot of systemic injustices I haven't faced, gate-keeping access in the workforce (and every other aspect of life). Like Jin said - we are all at different points on our path, and not everyone's path looks the same, so we shouldn't compare ourselves to people in a different part of their own journey.

It was not my first (or worst) existential crisis or bout of chronic depression, but just like always, to get out of it, I needed change - something new to distract myself with. So, I spent my days in job-limbo doing cheap freelance work for a failing food delivery service and consuming as much BTS content as my non-existent sleep schedule would allow. Then out of the blue, my boyfriend's boss sent me an offer for a full-time position. It felt like a miracle. I'm sorry for talking so much about myself and not nearly enough about BTS... but my point is, what everyone says is true. BTS finds you when you need them most - and then you grow together.

Over the last four years, I have done a lot of growing - got a house, got married, adopted the two sweetest shelter cats I've ever met, become a proper front-end developer, become a volunteer mentor for students, and learned a lot about self-worth. Those last two, I mostly owe to BTS and ARMY. It's amazing what some positive examples and a sense of community can do for a person. Of course, my husband is wonderful - he is my best friend, but my messed-up brain makes it really hard to believe that the nice things he says to me are objectively true, and not just because he loves me. The support and validation I have felt from other ARMY and the kind, insightful messages from BTS have helped me so much.

Over three years with the 'miracle' job, I learned to do as much as I could - user experience, e-commerce setup, project management, I even stepped in to cover help support and dev team members. More importantly, I learned to recognize when I was being used. With strength and encouragement from BTS and ARMY, I stopped thinking things like "I'm just lucky to have this job" or "I understand someone else needed that raise more". I recognized when my boss tried to gaslight me, got mad when he said my husband made enough for both of us, and realized that company needed me more than I needed them.

I looked for new jobs and found something more stable, more honest (with employees & clients), and much better paying with a considerably lighter workload. I did feel guilty about leaving - but I left anyway, because I had slowly learned that I matter too, and it's ok to want things. When you grow up in a household where there isn't enough money for wants, and the needs of others are more important, you just stop thinking about yourself.

It's no one's fault really, but un-learning internalized belittlement is incredibly difficult. I still catch myself sometimes - feeling selfish for even simple things, like mentioning where I want to eat. I can't express how much the songs 'Tomorrow' then 'Paradise' and now 'Black Swan' mean to me - BTS' discography has been like therapy, and their speeches, livestreams, random words of affirmation, and personal stories have encouraged me so profoundly. They have helped me discover so many things about myself and taught me a new kind of love. I only hope the things I can do as an ARMY allow me to give back even a fraction of the life they have given me.

People refer to adolescence as the 'formative years' and sure, that is a crucial time - but I think any period of significant change or growth can be just as impactful. I would certainly classify my time with BTS as 'formative years'. I am learning to be a better me, a better partner, and a better human. I don't know what this world will look like in 30 years, where I will be living, or what my job will be - but I know I'll still be ARMY. When the bright lights and roaring cheers are nothing more than echoes of my memories, 'bangtan' will live on. I will carry this art, this music, this magic with me forever. Wherever those seven amazing people are - whatever they are doing, I will continue to support them as they have supported me.

ABOUT ME - @narwhalzipan

I am 28 years old, and work from home as a Web Administrator for 100+ banks & credit unions. I'm married and we have a dog & two cats. Yoongi is my unofficial bias - OT7 all the way. I like soft & fuzzy things, art of every form - especially woodblock prints, dark humor, weird history, and comfort food.

BTS Brings Magic Into My Life!

Hello, my name is Lynn. My Army Twitter is Whisper1204! I am 42 years old and an ARMY Mom. I was born and raised in the Philippines and live in Canada. How did I discover BTS? I saw BTS in 2017 on Ellen's Show. Back then, I wasn't interested. In 2018, my eldest daughter started to talk to me about them, and how great and talented they were. She wanted to attend a concert in Hamilton, Ontario. I didn't let her go the concert (yup, I'm so mean). Fast forward - May 2019, I'm on vacation in the Philippines when my eldest daughter tells me that her Dad bought her a BTS album, MOTS Persona. It catches my attention; my husband is very cheap, and he taught our kids between wants and needs. For him to buy the album shows how important it was for my daughter. I came back from my vacation, and my daughter was so excited to tell me about BTS. I saw the spark in her eyes when she's talked about them. She told me how much BTS inspired her. I slowly opened my ears about BTS to get close and get connected to my daughter.

Saturday, July 13, 2019, I watched the first MV that stole my heart, "Blood Sweat and Tears." I started searching for them in YT; I watched their acceptance speech on MAMA 2018 and cried. That whole weekend I watched BTS videos until I fell asleep. I knew at the moment I loved this group and understood why my daughter loved them. I started following them on Twitter in my personal account. Like some of us, I was lurking around the fandom when I first started. I think it was August 2019; my daughter brought me to watch the BTS documentary, "Bring the Soul, The Movie," in the theatre. She brought me to a cup sleeves event in Toronto for Namkook, Jimin, Jin, V, and Jhope. I realized she's not ashamed to be with me. As the days went by, we got closer and closer. She started openly telling me about her personal life. She even chose to go out with me rather than her friends. BTS brought my daughter back to my life. Now she's saving money for both of us for a trip to South Korea. She's excited about it. I'm so excited about it.

August 2020, I got sick, and in and out of the hospital. Due to the COVID restrictions, nobody could be with me in the ER. I only had BTS music and my Twitter friends with me cheering me up. I didn't feel alone at that moment.

September 2020, I decided to do a bookmark giveaway in honour of Namjoon's birthday. In the same month, I had a blood transfusion that I was allergic to, and they rushed me to the Trauma Centre. When I woke up, I asked the nurse about my phone. She asked me if the phone has a photo of a man holding a dog. She then said, "Is this your son?" I smiled and said it's a BTS member named V and his dog Yeontan. I told her about them, and another nurse came in and said, "Oh, you looked happy." A few hours ago, I was on the brink of death, but BTS has this magic effect on us, right? I was admitted for a whole week after that incident. When I went home, the bookmark making gave me a reason to get up in the morning. I gathered all my energy so I could continue sending bookmarks to ARMY around the world.

October 2020, my treatment started, and I discovered I have a heart problem on top of it. During my stay in the hospital, BTS music comforted me; their videos made me laugh, their messages empowered me, and they are all gorgeous, I can't deny. My ARMY friends played a big part in my recovery, too. They continuously encouraged me to live. I found a family in the fandom. It's been 635 days since BTS became part of my daily life. These are the days I feel blessed to have my family, friends, Army friends, and BTS on my side. Whatever life throws at me, I know I can handle it because I have them.

For those ARMY who received my bookmarks, please know I appreciate you a lot. The bookmark you received represents my courage to live. To BTS, thank you for your existence in my life; I am grateful for the 7 of you every day. To my daughter, I owe all of this to you.

I love you, Babe!

BT21 Characters

KOYA: RM

RJ: JIN

Mang: J-Hope

Chimmy: JIMIN

Cooky: JUNGKOOK

Shooky: SUGA

Tata: V

Van: ARMY

A Traumatic Time

Hi! My name is Empress (not my real name), I discovered BTS around 2015-2016. I was in an abusive marriage, the abuse started after I caught my husband cheating. I left him after 2 years of enduring it. I became depressed and thought that my marriage falling apart, and my husband cheating was all my fault, and this lasted for months. One day I just wanted to forget everything, so I got my phone and just scrolled thru social media. While scrolling I saw a picture of 7 smiling boys. I was intrigued because the way they smiled were different, the smiles I saw were genuine, I couldn't explain it at that time. But seeing their smiles were like a ray of sunshine for me. I got curious, googled them immediately and found out they were a kpop group called BTS. So, I started listening to their music, I didn't understand a word they were saying but I liked their voices, and the beat of their music was so good that I was bopping my head to them. Next thing I know I was watching their MVs, their dances, looking up their names, etc. After a few months, my family noticed a difference in me, they said I started talking to them again, smiling and they can even sometimes hear me singing or see me dancing in my room. As time went on I fell in love with these 7 boys who made me smile again. Whenever I hear their songs or see their videos I feel happy. I love them not only for their songs but also for who they are. They have shown me that not all bad things that happen in our lives are bad (if that makes

방탄소년단

sense to you), because we learn from them, we grow with them, and it makes us stronger and better. For me, it made me realize that I am capable of being independent and that I am a strong person and a person that should be respected. That there is nothing wrong with loving myself. To this day I still love BTS, and I will never stop loving them and supporting them. I am forever grateful that I found them at the time when I needed them the most. I am forever ARMY.

Thank you 방탄소년단 . Borahae 💜

The Best Worst Moments in Life

If I were to go back to the beginning I wouldn't know where to start, really. Growing up as a kid, music always excited me. I didn't really have a preference and loved anything as long as it made me happy. Fairly recently I've discovered the song that I cherished so much as a child and surprisingly it was a kpop song by the legendary, Girl's Generation.

I'll be ashamed to say that my little cousin introduced me to BTS. They always loved singing Fake Love and that made me like the song too. However, I made the mistake of not really acknowledging the artist of the song. Fast forward a year later. I made friends with a guy who loved the group, he would always talk about Park Jimin, and I found it so cute, but again I just brushed it off. Despite this, the universe had different plans because once more while watching a tv show, BTS appeared. This made me stop and realize maybe these moments were signs and I should check them out. Being so busy with school, life, and finances I didn't have the time to do so sadly.

Well, it wasn't until everything didn't go as planned for me. I had entered a very toxic relationship that left me heartbroken.

During that period, I too found out that two people I've cherished for years and who I considered to be sisters weren't really who they said to be. It was heartache after heartache, and I began to put up this facade that I was okay. No one around me questioned a thing and would describe me as being bubbly and so outgoing. I was hurting. I really was with no one to talk to.

Freshman year was something that I always looked forward to and just like that everything went the wrong way. It wasn't until one morning while binge watching videos on Facebook that I came across a BTS boy with luv performance. I really loved the song and Taehyung's blue hair really drew me in. After reading so many positive comments about the group I went straight to Google with the idea that, "I just want to know the name of the blue-haired guy."

Oh, but that one Google search played the role of a leaping pad that would soon launch me into the world of excitement and self-love. I went from wanting to know their names to funny compilations and by the end of the day I was hooked. I can still remember me trying to recite the fan chant for the first time and getting angry every time I missed a name. Around the time I had no idea of the apps BTS had, I really just watched their YouTube channel but oh was I in for a treat once I heard about the multiple platforms.

The worst moments of my life soon began to turn into the best moments. In a way I am glad that those moments happened. It led me to so many friends and 7 individuals who understood me and wanted to change me. I am who I am today because of BTS and the best version of myself. I would give BTS the world if I can because they changed mine for the better.

Although I haven't attended a concert in person yet I'm happy that I attended many online ones and the most memorable one for me was the BangBangCon 24hr YouTube Concert. Fellow ARMYs were so kind to me in teaching and helping me navigate through everything and I cried during the concert because to me it was my first ever concert with the guys and it was great.

I wanted to share my experience to let you know that all things happen in your life for a reason. The worst moment in your life can lead you to the best moment. If you love something don't be afraid to express your love for it. Although many people would tease and ridicule you it can never overpower the love and faith BTS has in you. If you are willing and able to love 7 guys who you've never met before then you are able to love yourself. Back then I didn't know how to love myself but with the help of Kim Namjoon, Kim Seokjin, Min Yoongi, Jung Hoseok, Park Jimin, Kim Taehyung and Jeon Jungkook I learned that self-love is the best love and broken things are still beautiful. Thank BTS, my voice, my heart, my love and my best friends.

Kedysha

New Life With BTS

Hey!! I want to share how BTS changed my life So, to start, I've got to tell you about a little history of my life. I really hope you can read this, because this memory is the most precious thing I have.
I am 25 years old and since I was 3 months old I was diagnosed with atopic dermatitis. That's a health problem that totally destroys the self-esteem of all carriers 'cause we always have a scaling body and wounds, and in my case, it mainly affects my face.
So, throughout my life I had to deal with the fear of people seeing me in times of crisis 'cause I didn't want them to feel sorry for me. I always asked God every day why I couldn't be like all the other girls.
So, in 2013, I'd been through one of the worst times of my life. My father, separated from my mother. He was one of the people who had never seen me in times of allergic crisis. But a week before he died, and for the first time, I had the courage to let him see me. Three days later, I found out, that day was my last moment with him. It was very special, and I remember he said that if he could, he would give his life for me so that I wouldn't suffer like that. But the day he passed away, I had the worst allergic crisis of my life and didn't have the courage to say goodbye to him on his funeral. After that moment I still had to giving up many things and go through others for fear that the world would know a me with atopic dermatitis.
Today, I can tell you, I'm a new person and BTS has helped me a lot in this process, with all their messages about how important is to love and accept myself. A great proof of this is that I'm sharing this story with you. So, now, we

finally arrived on my precious BTS memories. At the first BTS concert in Brazil on 2019, the life gave me the opportunity to learn one more lesson: when I was waiting in my sector, I saw a girl who had atopic dermatitis and she was in a very strong crisis, but SHE WAS THERE, in front of thousands of ARMYs, to see the boys!! She wasn't caring about what people would say or think of her.
So, that moment struck me so much, that it completely changed the way I see myself, and since that day I'm no longer ashamed of who I am and of letting other people see me. That was definitely the best day of my life!

Thank you for listening to my story. I don't know anything about you, but I hope you were happy reading this. Thank you so much for this incredible project.

Borahae 💜
tataelephant

Youth is Not Over

I became a BTS fan quite by chance. As a wife and mother of grown children, I thought that the fun and carefree feeling of youth was over. I've never been a part of any fandom and Twitter was just a pretty much unused account. It all started one summer when I started watching Kdramas. When I was a kid and young adult, I loved the artistry of Asian films and the story lines. Recently, I started watching again. One day while searching for my next Kdrama using YouTube, I ran across a Korean singer singing American gospel songs! They were darn good! That intrigued me, so I searched some more and found a Korean duo singing American R&B. They were good! One day while looking for some entertainment during Covid quarantine, I ran across these young men who were practicing a dance. The song was Boy With Luv! I was shocked! They could dance! There was one who had real swag, Jhope. They all did, really. One was so cute, Jimin! Two looked like twins, but could dance, Jungkook and V. They moved so fast that it was hard to focus on anyone. I wanted to know more about them! Then I saw "ON" Woaah! I was blown away! I became excited but scared! I mean, who could I share this with? Who would understand my affection for these

young men of a different culture, ethnicity, and country? Their music was fun, energetic, and sexy. I learned their names, eventually. Heartbeat, Epiphany, Serendipity, and Young Forever were the first to be added to my playlist. As I heard more, I added more! Now, I have entire albums and counting! Then I found ARMY on Twitter and felt a part of something magical! I looked forward to their next online concerts, next comeback, next Vlive! Friends and family didn't share in the interest, but they understood that I was serious enough to buy me Bangtan gifts for Christmas. The ARMY bomb was my first prized possession. I joined a ARMY group chat and feel that I have possibly found lifelong friends. My life is brighter, more fun because of those 7 wonderful, inspiring, angelic human beings. I felt I've turned back the clock. I can dance to their music (or try to) and be happy. I can laugh at their Run episodes and delight in their achievements! I can't pick one, so I have 7 biases. I can't wait to meet them in my first live concert. I am sure that there will be an ocean of purple tears on that day! Happy tears!

Borahae!   Athena2020

My ARMY Adventure

Annyeong :) My journey to becoming an ARMY is not the common story. My basis for saying this, is because ALL the ARMYs that I encountered either became an ARMY because of a song, or a member, or an event in their life.

For me, it was a different story...

I was going along with my daily "usual" life. And by "usual" life, I mean taking care of my family (because I am a stay-at-home mom), doing my chores and my errands. And in between my itinerary were two shows -- Kdramas and the Graham Norton Show (GNS). I had been a Kdrama addict since the "Boys Over Flowers" era and the GNS has kept me entertained because of his humor and hosting skills.

As we all know, our lovely boys appeared in the GNS. To be really honest, I kind of told myself that i wasn't going to patronize Kpop. This was because I had been hearing a lot of things about this industry. I wasn't happy with the information I got... that the Kpop idols were being mistreated and they work like crazy, almost like slaves. I had the impression that the Korean culture had parents brainwashing their kids that being a Kpop idol was the best thing they can become and if needed, they have to undergo surgery to become pretty. And worse, even at an early age.

So when I saw our boys perform at the GNS, I was indifferent with them. I wasn't liking or disliking them in anyway. Because for me, it was just another song number since the format of the show has been like that -- the guests are interviewed, they all have a good chat and in the last 15 minutes, there will be a song number and the artist will be interviewed on the couch. Little did I know that, THAT interview will turn things around. (laughing now at the memory of it kekekekekeke).

BTS wasn't new to my ears. Somehow, I heard about them, and I knew they were one of those kpop groups. But to my surprise, Graham started showing the TIME MAGAZINE cover, and a picture of our boys delivering a speech in the UN Assembly. Boy! I wish I could have taken a picture of myself that time, if only you could have seen my face!!! I was like..."Seriously? What's happening in this world? Has TIME MAG lowered their standards in choosing their covers? And UN?

But thanks to my "open-minded" character, I snapped at shocked me. And so I told myself, "Uh-uh girl...if TIME MAGAZINE branded them as "next generation leaders" and UN having them speak, Then there has to be something special about this group.

So, the first thing I did was watch their UN speech. Then, the random video that followed was their title medley in Wembley. After watching these two videos, I came to the conclusion that things weren't working. I mean, I am 50 years old and I am not the kind of person that gets hooked by just a good performance. Then VOILA!!! There it was. The random videos were all in front of me... By random videos, I mean the documentaries about them. So, I started watching them: "The Real BTS"; "BTS Hardships"; "Bring the Soul"; "Burn the Stage"; "Break the Silence", then their concert makings including their opening and ending comments, and more.

And that was it! After watching all these videos, all I had to say to myself was..."How can you not fall in love" with these kids. Yes, KIDS...Because that is how I love them...as a mom with seven wonderful sons.

I mean, really? How can you not love them? They are the most sincere, humble, true, honest, sweet, simple human beings I have ever seen. Pretending? Because they are in front of the camera? NO SIR. Because CONSISTENCY is the name of the game. A person can only pretend to a certain extent. The real one will surface in the long run because he will get tired of pretending eventually.

These are boys who know about social responsibility; they are boys who not only talk the talk but walk the walk.

So, what is BTS to me. BTS keeps me preoccupiedly happy. They are a great stress buster. Why? Because when I watch them, I become a complete LAT.

L= I laugh like crazy because they are effortlessly funny.

A= I am amazed and in awe at their wisdom, considering their age. They can be crackheads, but they know when and how to rise to the occasion. When it is time to get serious, they speak about lessons in life that inspires and encourages people.

T= I am touched by their bond. Not friendship, but bond. And I mean all of them. I wish people would stop making "romantic" notions about them. I mean, seriously, they are not gay and they are not in any relationship.

Taehyung already strongly spoke about this. And we are giving the haters a reason to lash at us with this shipping. I mean, if we ship them, ship for their sibling bromance. It is such a genuine and beautiful friend-family relationship. Let's not tarnish it.

So, that is my ARMY journey. I call it an adventure. In conclusion, let me just say, that I have never become a fan of any artist in my younger years. I like music, songs, and dances, but it was more of a "per song" basis. I actually think it's funny that I became a fan in my 50s. But then again, there is no age limit to appreciating talent and hard work, right? I only wish I could see them in person and tell them that I am thankful, that BTS happened in my lifetime. And always, I will be a proud mom for them... laughing at their antics, celebrating their success, and crying with them in their sadness. BORAHAE!!!

Juncel Marcial

BTS are my saviours

Hi BTS,

[Insert: fanchant] 😆

hello Jin, Suga, RM, J-Hope, Jimin, V, JK

I hope you guys are well, at you're best and happy. First off, I wish I could just place my heart onto this page to show you my feelings because I don't think any words could suffice for my ever-growing love for each one of you- you are my universe. Keep shining!

My name is Muaziz (yeah its hard to pronounce- say: mu-a-ziz- it comes from Arabic and it means well respected and originates from the word azeez, which means special/important)... lol sorry I'm waffling too much. I'm 19 (zodiac sign: Aries) - and I live in England, near the northwest in a small city called Preston - its a rather normal, boring place but, I'm so used to it now. Much of my childhood I spent moving around various cities, as my parents constantly worried over which school would best suit me and my siblings.. lol anyways, I grew up being the typical middle child, too young to do things like my older sibling, yet too old to be childish and be spoiled like my younger sister. Growing up, I struggled going out, I was too shy to speak, I was socially awkward, which to this day i still slightly am, I had self-conscious issues and I suffered from anxiety. Time flew, I became conditioned to my nature and accepted it - like it was just who I was. While everybody else around me would talk around in high school, I preferred to stay quit and to myself. Around this time, my family went through many crisis and we lost many precious souls, along with that I started to suffer from a lack of sleep as well developing sleep paralysis. I became frustrated with myself and just didn't see the fun in anything. I loved studying, especially history, art, and literature and even though I worked hard and tried to pull myself together, everything felt pointless, and it just made me feel so worthless. Although I did have friends who I could talk to, I just couldn't bring myself to share my misery with them. A couple of weeks into year 8 in high school, my parents were called in- I was too scared to tell my dad but eventually the teacher got through to him and asked him to come in to see her. She was worried that I was too quiet in class, not participating and thought that if I continued like this, it would be unlikely for me to achieve good gcse grades (exams taken in year 11 in the UK, before college). Deep down, I knew my parents were disappointed -maybe they had lost belief in me too. That day, I broke down, I cried at my situation and that was the day I promised to myself that it was time I do some good for myself. From then on, I began to work hard, despite my struggles, especially in maths, which I hated. Time flew, while I busied myself in studying, I came to year 11, the year I sat my gcse exams- I was dreading it. I would stress out at the smallest of things and was exhausted and confused. One day, in late spring 2019, while I was in class, a girl behind me was talking about someone called Jin. Being an already quite person, I continued listening to her conversation in silence. I figured out that she was arguing with another girl in class, who was poking fun at her listening to kpop. At that time, I didn't pay much attention, which I to this day regret (I would have found you sooner if I had known 😭). I continued the next couple of weeks, very stressed about upcoming exams and things were too busy to do anything besides revision for exams. I suffered from a lot of sleep paralysis around this time, to a point that I just hated sleeping. One weekend, Jin came up on my mind, so I decided to search him up - after all, who is this guy?? Little did I know it would be our WWH!!

When I searched for Jin, my heart went boom boom! For the first time in years, I felt soo happy, he just looked sooo comforting to me. I spent around 1 hour just looking through Google images, slowly slowly, other beautiful faces appeared, and I was like wooah! My god who are these guys? I quickly then went on YouTube and typed in BTS songs, my first ever BTS song thus became 'Fake love', which I still love soo much with all my heart. I realized I was missing something I should have found earlier, I cried at the lyrics as it slowly hit me that all along up until that moment, I was hurting, yet pretending I was strong and the lyrics deeply touched my heart - like all of you were personally telling me 'it will be ok'. I knew then that I'd found something I could hold onto and would never let go - you were a gift from God on my rainiest day! Thank you for coming to me BTS. I began to watch fmvs, comedy skits and interviews and I slowly began to learn about all your amazing souls. I was sooo excited and happy that I decided to have my sisters join me in a BTS watch party. Despite all my troubles at home and anxiety of exams, I began to love listening to music, I looked forward to sleeping every night just so I could finally relax and watch BTS. I realized that despite all my troubles, there was still some hope. Thank you RM for teaching me to love myself and Jimin, thank you for showing me that hard work pays off and to always follow my dreams! Time flew, exams were done, and results day came! I wasn't looking forward to it. I remember listening to Moonchild while going to pick my results and I just felt better- pretended I had someone besides me who had my back. Omg! And you won't believe what I got! I was over the moon, I had achieved way more than I thought I would, with 100% on both my English literature papers! I remember just feeling so so so delighted and I thanked my lucky stars for bringing BTS to me. Lol, I remember also pretending that I'd go up to RM to share my results and thinking he'd be so proud! Anyways, fast forward to summer - which was the best summer ever! I vibed to all your songs beginning from your first ever album. I cried at some songs and laughed along with you on BTS run. My ultimate bias became Jimin! Of course, it's sooo hard to decide because I'm always getting bias wrecked by each one of you at different point... Jimin I love

you so so so much! Plz let us know what shampoo you use because your hair is just wow! JK became my official bias wrecker! What's with you getting soooo huge these days though? 😅 I'm just sooo happy like I've never been, I'm glad I found you as well as my galaxy of all other ARMYs. Seeing all you're trials since 2013 and proving the haters wrong as well as all your patience and hard work over the years has taught me so much! I began to dream high and thought that if BTS can, so will I. I decided I'd work really hard in college and set my mind to studying medicine at uni. I then started college in 2020, where I studied chemistry, biology and literature. College was tough, yet I was working really hard! I saw how far I'd come - I wasn't the old me anymore, it was still the me, yet stronger. Even though I was still socially awkward and still shy, I saw that I had gained much more confidence and self-love than my previous years. I slowly began to open up to new people, I met many ARMYs, who to this day I still hold close and love very much. Talking to ARMYs made me feel safe and I realized they were just like me - we were all a big family, each a shining star in the dark night sky - our own Mikrokosmos. Together we spazzed over you. I met many Yoongi stans, many other Jimin stans, J-Hope stans, Jin stans, JK stans and of course both my sisters who themselves had become ARMYs too - one who stans V and the other RM. Sometimes it hits me how far you are - like all the way in Korea,
  yet I still feel you're love radiating all the way through to my own little home, in my own little city. I'm going to admit, there's emotional times where I'll just cry as it hits me, that you're half

a world apart, just like I am doing now, I often look at the sky, thinking at least we're under the same sky, sun, moon, and stars and maybe, just maybe right now you're looking up too and so are all other ARMYs. I see BTS and ARMYs now as my second family, who I'd never let go of, not even when I'm down my last breath. The past few years have been a long ride, a long adventure to finding myself in you. I'm so glad I've met so many ARMYS along the way, who all love you just like I do. I have now finished college and waiting for my ALEVEL grades... and hell yeck! I bet I've done good hopefully. Thanks Yoongi for teaching me to be savage and to love that side of myself too. I now have big dreams and something that I'm always reminded of is what you, RM taught us: 'in order to love others, you should begin by loving yourself". .Just like how one cannot pour from an empty glass and sincerely President Kim my respects and hats off to you and you're clever intellect! You're sincerely the man! Don't blame me when I proudly say that thanks to you, I have now developed what is termed as "the daddy issues".

Moving on to my favourite BTS song, of course I love every single one, though fake love will be the one I hold close, since that was the one that reincarnated me into an ARMY. Mikrokosmos would be next- it's just pure love for ARMY and it just makes me soo happy to be part of the fandom, followed by Seesaw and then Sea (I cried so bad to sea) , oh yeah then No More Dream and coffee too. I love Jin's Abyss, all of Jimin's solos, RM's

Moonchild will always be my fav, Suga's Daechwita, JHope's Hope World, V's... ughhh its soooo hard to decide but basically I love every single song, that goes for all the members solos, but the ones mentioned are ones that are most memorable to me. Finally, JK, still with you... ah I can just imagine you confessing love to your girl while singing this and sitting at a piano. JK I've done so many cover and duets with you, it's sincerely become a hobby now. Anyways I hope, whoever your better halves turn out to be, love you passionately for all that you deserve. I hope you're happy couples together!
💜💜💜💜💜💜💜

Yeah and I'm still waiting/dreaming about the day when I'll get to meet you guys face to face ...it seems a long way off, but I guess there are no debts to wishful dreaming right? I'm also so broke that I've never got a single album, or even an ARMY bomb, I've never attended a fan sign neither joined a live muster... the only thing I have is a purple heart, so I'm sending lots of love and hugs to all 7 of you and to all the ARMYs out there. I promise, I shall get an album very soon....

I feel there's soo much more to tell you guys, but I guess that's most of it to my very still life. Oh yeah forgot to mention, my hobbies are:

Tuning in to BTS VLives and run episodes,

reading, watching kdramas... (recently watching Vincenzo and Youth of May), watching Tik Tok edits of BTS, watching YouTube skits of BTS, sketching, writing poems, lying around like a potato, listening to BTS songs (obviously), karaoke and listening to slowed down sad songs (yeah I'm a sado).

I'm eating chocolate and drinking jasmine tea! I know I shouldn't be eating late at night it's unhealthy... it's ok though, today can just be an exception. 😌 😊 Seriously try that, it's soooo relaxing! I'm listening to Serendipity slowed down in the background. It just feels great this moment, there's a soft breeze outside and the curtains are fluttering about, and I just feel so great typing away... I'm talking to all 7 of you, I've never felt this comfortable, excited and happy all at once.

I'd like to also request if we could get an era where the rap and vocal line swap roles... I'd love to hear Jimin rap !!!! Aaaah, just like in Tony Montana!! Aah, that would be a dream come true. I'd love to hear more of JHope, RM and Suga singing. Seriously, all if you have such sweet melodious voices, you give us sooo much love and always perform at your best, Seriously, we don't deserve so much love. Myself and on behalf of all other ARMYS I'd like to say a big heartfelt thank you from the bottom of our hearts for always loving ARMYS and taking us along with you on all your adventures! It's been a long yet fun journey and no matter where the road will lead, even if it's a dead end, we know that BTS have our backs and just know that ARMYS have yours. We all love all 7 of you so so soo much, plz take care, stay safe and happy until we meet again. Also, if you ever feel upset, exhausted, and tired, we're here for you, plz show us when you're sad or angry and don't hide it just because you feel ARMYs shouldn't see that side of you. Did I mention that I love you so much? Now stop and smile, you've done great today - go treat yourself!

Leaving off with a song recommendation: Don't You Worry by Oh Wonder and Another Love by Tom Odell (try the slowed down versions).

Also, I think i should try going to sleep now... it is now 3:16AM here 🥺😬.....

OK BYEEE TAKE care of each other for ARMYs! Let's meet soon!

💜💜💜💜💜💜💜👻 bye 🥺🥰

MB

ARMY

J-HOPE

SUGA

TAE TAE

Jimin

Joon

Jin

Kookie

BTS Saved Me: A Time of Learning to Love Myself

Where do I even begin? BTS, a band that I would have never thought in a million years, that I would be interested in. And yet, a co-worker simply suggested a song - Fake Love to be exact. After watching the music video, I was hooked. It was then I found Spring Day, and from that moment on, I knew I was in for the long haul. I started to stan the boys on Feb. 18th, 2019.

Many people wonder what is so great about the stigma or exactly why BTS is so popular today? How can a Korean boy band, a group of 7 amazing, talented souls brought together by fate touch the very souls of ARMY internationally? It's a common saying between fellow fans alike that BTS tends to find you when you really need them - and it is 1000000% true.

It's hard to put into full words of how much these men have changed my life, into something so beautiful. So, I will try my best to tell my story.

I was 22 years old and worked a retail job that I hated. I had a lot of struggles with terrible management at my place of employment and how they treated their staff. My best friend of almost 8 years at that time had moved several hours away. I was lacking close immediate friends. My one co-worker at the time suggested I check the boys out. And I was hooked

the moment I watched several videos. I had been fighting depression, yet I had not been truthful to my family and friends about what I was truly feeling emotionally. On top of my depressive thoughts, I had feelings of self-doubt and self-image issues that have been present with me all the way back to when I was bullied in middle school for my weight. Things were not in my favor this year, and it was only going to get worse as the year progressed.

June 2019 was a summer I will never forget. I lost a family dog, a golden retriever named Tucker, who had grown up with me, from undiagnosed stomach cancer. It was such a hard loss for me to process, but I kept listening to BTS. As I continued my journey, I felt connected to them. Interestingly enough, it was only days when Jin released "This Night" and I bawled my eyes out. It was almost like I had found BTS and when I needed comfort, there was Jin singing the words of understanding. It would only be several months later that 2020 would come around, and we would have a second unexpected loss, our sweet Sadie who was a black Boxador.

2020 was a year for everyone that was hard, but it was the hardest year for me to overcome. My depression had hit an all-time low. I had thoughts of just giving up and letting go. After losing 2 family dogs who were like my siblings to me, the COVID pandemic, losing my job temporarily, watching the racism and bigotry spike in my country, I had been ready to throw in the towel.

But something in me told me to hang on. I kept listening and watching the boys. I spent more time on twitter, meeting and connecting with other ARMY. Watching the live concerts that the boys put on for us. They were the thing that gave me hope. I listen to their music, and the lyrics, the raw emotion hits me in no other way than anything has ever hit before. BTS are more than a "boy band" that just release music. They care about ARMY, they love their fans and they always put 100% of themselves in everything that they do. Their work ethic, their love of speaking up on important issues, standing against bullying, their own individual passions. Everything about them in authentic. I connect with each member on a different level, and I admire them all. I feel as if I am growing up with them since they are all close to my age.

My now 24-year-old self, in 2021 can look back, happily and realize that BTS is more than just a band, more than just music or entertainment. They are real people with emotions, who care and are so humble, honest, and hardworking. They are able to connect with their fans in ways most celebrities disregard nowadays. I am in such a better place and mindset. I started

to learn the process of loving myself and being patient with myself. They have brought me on a journey that I am still learning, and I hope that I will continue to meet amazing ARMY and friends on this ride. Namjoon, Jin, Yoongi, Hoseok, Jimin, Taehyung, Jungkook; I want to say thank you, for being your goofy, amazing selves. No amount of words could ever describe the love and admiration I have for you. You saved me. You were there for me when I needed you most. So, like you sing: "You gave me the best of me, so you give you the best of you." I wish you nothing but the best. It's only up from here.

I love you boys, and I love ARMY. Thank you for taking the time and reading. Please know that things do get better, and that people come into your lives at times when you need them, and they might be people who you would never suspect. So let that door open in your heart. That is what makes our universe so magical and beautiful.

Borahae,
Sarah

My Life Before BTS

I had no goal, ambition, emotions in life. I still remember the year 2017, the first time I had entered the college. I changed the subject from the one which I could give my life to, to one where I had no interest. It seemed as if I was nothing but shell. My bestie saw the changes in me daily I had struggled so far to get into this university to major in history, but I changed just because I thought I don't deserve history. Well to add, I had also undergone the worst breakup with my 6-year relationship. He was hurting me, so I had no self-confidence and love. I gave my everything only to discover he cheated on me with another girl.

Yes I was suicidal. I just closed myself in the shell of mine not wanting to speak to strangers for they all were happy and satisfied. I could have died for I tried to quit at least few times. Now my friend had had enough and tried to help me in different ways. One of them was music. She asked me to listen and played on my guitar. I really don't know how but I came across the song, Dope. My first reaction was, who are they, whoever they were, it was nice. Then came the song that motivated me to not to give up and struggle hard to work for them, for my mom and myself. Well, the song was Tomorrow.

Well, I don't know if this small letter will get to you or not, but I would sincerely like to thank you for making my life happier, better, and giving me the confidence to face life and myself. Thank you for giving me the zeal to never give up and work hard. Thank you for being my sunshine and light and reason to continue living.

Well now I am a student who is going to get her MA in history next year.

Keerthu

BTS saved me

Music has always been an important part of my life. I was always in the choir and I played the flute for about 10 years through school. My first "group crush" was The Monkees! Yes, I know, most of you are asking who? My name is Vickie, and I am 66 years young. I first saw BTS when they were very young. I don't remember what show they were on or what song they sang and danced to, but I remember I liked them! But as life goes, mine got unbelievably busy with my mother's illness and baby grandchildren. Somewhere in there, along with my family, I started listening to country music.

Fast forward to March 30, 2020. BTS was on a show hosted by James Corden. The pandemic had just started, and they were quarantined together in SK. They performed in one of their practice rooms, but they were awesome! They sang and danced their hearts out to BOY WITH LUV, and I fell in "LUV" instantly even though I couldn't understand a word they said. They were all amazing performers, but I couldn't take my eyes off the tall, thin one all in black! JK is still my bias to this day!

I needed to know their names and all I could find out

through the pandemic!

about them. It didn't take long, and I fell hard and fast down the rabbit hole! I thought I would have a hard time with the quarantine, and my whole family felt the same way, but for me, it was just the opposite. I heard a lot of people were having trouble with depression and anxiety, however, I enjoyed staying home! I had so much BTS music to listen to and so much to read about them that I was having a good time! I watched RUN episodes and concerts on our fire stick! All my family (husband, two daughters, sister, and grandchildren) agree that BTS saved me through the pandemic! I found BTS and an ARMY of new friends just when I needed them! The last several months have been the happiest! IBIS (my Twitter DM) has made me feel welcome and now they are part of my family too. 💜 There is no better feeling!

JK Fan

The Gift of BTS

On New Year's Eve 2017 my 11-year-old middle child found BTS. Never one to shy away from things unique and different, she entered 2018 and the BTS rabbit hole full throttle. Watching from an acceptable mom-distance, I tried not to cramp her style, but asked her to play songs as we traveled that summer. She'd talk excitedly about the entire group, her bias V, and the music. When BTS' October 2018 show at Citifield was announced, taking place the day before her 12th birthday, I knew going to the concert together would be the perfect gift for her. What I didn't know, was that I'd receive a gift as well.

To prepare for the concert I tried to learn the members' names, and the fan chant. That night at the stadium we sat next to a woman my age with a version one ARMY bomb and a Suga picket. When BTS took the stage, ARMY bombs alight, I watched my child transform. Her joy was pure and contagious. I had never seen anything like it. My daughter had found herself a massive, positive, multi-generational, international community centered around music I didn't know existed. BTS' performance was incredible and their ending - inspiring. I wasn't quite ready to call myself ARMY, but I could tell I was leaving a different person from who I was entering the stadium's gates that night.

Wondering if there really were adult ARMY, like the woman with the Suga picket, I joined a few online groups and read and watched everything about BTS that I could find. Three years later, I am a Suga bias myself. I fell in love with the group's artistry, and sincerity. I attended more BTS concerts and exhibitions and began to make ARMY friends and pen-pals. When the pandemic hit, I further realized that not only does BTS' music provide comfort and consolation to

ARMY, but ARMY provides comfort and consolation to each other. I can't imagine how dark 2020 might have been if I didn't have BTS, the opportunity to watch MOTS: One and BangBangCon with my daughter, or the "happy mail" my ARMY friends and I send to each other. A professional artist, I started making BTS fan art here and there. I began collecting enamel pins and supporting other ARMY artists.

Up until then, being an "ARMY Mom," supporting my child and her interests, was safe. Being an adult ARMY independent from my child, brought on a different reaction. Some people in my life made snide comments about a person my age liking a "boy band." Others said nothing, while still thinking I was weird. But like the lyrics from Never mind, I have, after 40+ years of living, decided to live how I want, guided by my own beliefs. The result is a smarter, braver, happier, me. I am more creative at work and in life. I took two semesters of college level Hangul and Korean language this past year and amazed myself with what I can do if I set my mind to it.

I thought discovering BTS would be a story of a mother learning from, and growing closer to, her daughter. It has most certainly been that, but it's also a story of unexpected growth and empowerment for me. I now let myself be unabashedly inspired by BTS and their lyrics, because just like my daughter joyfully lighting up at the first few notes of Citifield, I eventually realized BTS's music lights me up too. And that spark, is BTS' gift to all ARMY.

daydreeem

Blood, Sweat and what??

Hello ARMY and all reading this. My name is Wendie. A 40 yr old who comes from a little town in Ontario, Canada. BTS found me in 2016 when I was at one of my lowest points ever. I suffer from PTSD due to childhood trauma. I was adopted at the age of 8 into an amazingly loving and kind family but what had happened to me in my early years and what I had to deal with has left its marks permanently etched into my being. Because of my PTSD I have depression, anxiety, and panic attacks. I struggle to sleep, with migraines and other health issues and daily life can be a challenge. Anyone who deals with any of these issues knows how time consuming it can be. How it can take over your daily life until you become a shell of who you want to be, who you used to be and who you strive to be. I was working as a chef in an amazing restaurant that strived to cook locally grown and organic food. We were known across Canada as "The Greenest Restaurant in Canada". If that alone wasn't enough pressure, being a female chef is also a huge pressure in and of itself. We tend to have to work twice as hard to get anywhere. But I digress. In 2014 I lost my younger sister to a house fire. In 2015 my brother was killed. So, by the time 2016 came around I couldn't handle much of anything anymore. My nerves were shot, I was having almost daily anxiety attacks, I had to leave stores, family events etc., multiple times because I was panicking and/or I'd find somewhere to hide (in clothing racks, bathrooms, and under tables). I was working 60-70h a week to keep my mind busy and so I wouldn't have much of any free time and then I finally collapsed. My Doctor told me "No more, you are killing yourself and your body can't handle it anymore". She put me on ODSP (disability) and told me that very likely I wouldn't be able to go back to work. My body had had enough. My hands gave out, I had almost constant migraines, barely sleeping, was sick and in pain all the time. I lost my career which I loved and felt like I had lost my reason to live. I gave up. I was done. Then BTS hit me. I was going through YouTube and came across Blood Sweat & Tears. I had heard of BTS but other than looking up who they were, saw they were all younger than me and figured meh... ~~Not my thing~~ they are too young.

I didn't pay any attention to them.

But for some reason this time I thought what the heck. Listened to Blood Sweat & Tears, then listened again, then closed my eyes and listened again. I was hooked. Their voices felt like they were caressing my heart and my head. I felt excited about something. So I spent the next few days listening to anything and everything I could find about BTS. Both good and bad. I Googled each member, the group, watched everything I could on YouTube (again both good and bad) I was hooked. But I was a little scared to admit to anyone I was in-love with a "Boy-Band" from South Korea. (I've always had a fascination with Asian Culture, especially South Korea and China) I joined a Facebook group and sat in the background watching. Then in 2018 I opened a Twitter account. Again, sitting in the background until I felt comfortable enough to contact some ARMY. ARMY honestly terrified me until this point. They were so passionate, so powerful (Boy how I wish I had been braver earlier). I found some groups I was comfortable with, joined voting tags, stayed up all night just to watch award shows, laughed and cried watching Bon Voyage, Run BTS etc. Now in 2021, I am a VERY proud ARMY (I tell anyone and everyone whoever you are) with some of THE MOST AMAZING ARMY friends who I consider family. People I have grown to care about so much and this is all due to 7 amazing South Korean men who found me when I was at my lowest point and ready to end everything. I may be be alone in my little town/area "stanning" BTS, but I do not regret it AT ALL. Kim Namjoon, Kim Seokjin, Min Yoongi, Jung Hoseok, Park Jimin, Kim Taehyung and Jeon Jungkook, you literally pulled me out of the darkness and showed me the light. You showed me that it is okay to feel down sometimes but we shouldn't live there. You gave me a family in ARMY who support me no matter what. You love me for who I am because being your ARMY is enough. Thank you for saving me, for giving me a Home because when I think of BTS, I think of Home. I love you more than love.

Goldilocks81

Beautiful, Timely, Special: My Journey with BTS

BEAUTIFUL!

It all started with 'Butterfly'. I first heard the song on a Korean music show, sung by Hyolyn, a former member of the South Korean group, Sistar. I was hooked by its melancholic melody and although the only words that I understood from the lyrics were 'like a butterfly', I was captivated by it. There is something so painfully soothing about it. 'Whose song is this? Why is it so beautiful?' I asked my daughter, whose knowledge of Kpop music was certainly more diverse than mine. She replied, 'BTS!' and that's all it took. My journey of discovery began.

The curiosity to find out who the original artists were led me from one video to another. Soon, I was spending hours getting to know their names, ages, personalities, and other endearing qualities. I found myself laughing at their antics and crying while understanding their lyrics. My heart swelled looking at how much they adore and respect each other. I found myself rooting for them in award shows like they are my family. I looked for books I could read about them. I found inspiration from their speeches, interviews and background stories and I have used them during some of my lessons in class.

Yes, these seven gentlemen are gorgeous, but to me, what makes them stand apart from the rest is the honesty in their musical journey and the healing messages in their songs. As I go deeper into discovering who BTS is, I took the time to listen to their entire discography and learnt the meaning behind each and every song. I read the book 'BTS: The Review – A Comprehensive Look at the Music of BTS' by music critic Kim Youngdae to have a more in depth understanding of the music. With every search I made and every song I listened to, I realized my respect and love for these talented young men grew exponentially. How do these men stay rooted and humble? How do they find the courage to address controversial issues and yet be relatable and connected to their listeners? How do they pull people of different ages, genders, ethnicities and cultures together through their songs?

TIMELY!

Every day I feel blessed to have found BTS at the time when I needed them the most. I was struggling to find a sense of purpose and peace then. I needed an escape from a challenging period of my life. BTS provided that solace.

Getting to know them gave me a sense of happiness and at the same time, made me rethink the choices I have to make in my life. Being lost in their music somehow gave me clarity. BTS also gave my daughters and I opportunities to bond and 'fangirl'. We were over the moon when we managed to grab tickets to their concert in Singapore in January 2019. We can't speak Korean much, but we sang our hearts out (never mind if the lyrics were wrong) and waved our ARMY bombs with pride. A surreal and magnificent moment indeed! With the current pandemic and the uncertainty of when live concerts can resume, that concert became more and more precious to me.

SPECIAL!

Over time, every ARMY will realize that the bond we have with BTS and fellow ARMY around the world is very special and unique. We may not know everyone personally, but the camaraderie we have is tight. We move in great precision when it comes to supporting BTS, be it streaming their music, participating in charitable causes or even protecting them against discrimination. I have made friends with ARMY from different parts of the world and that is made possible because of our love for BTS.

There are many musical acts that I listen to and love but only BTS felt this special. Their achievements speak volumes of their talent and their passion in what they do. They have earned their rightful place in the history of music, and they have definitely made a significant presence in my life.

absolutred16

borahae - 보라 해 - I purple you

saranghae - 사랑해 - I love you

kamsahamnida - 감사합니다 - Thank you

bangtansonyeondan - 방탄소년단 - BTS

annyeonghaseyo - 안녕하세요 - hello

jwesonghamnida - 죄송합니다 - sorry

Jeogiyo - 저기요 - Excuse me

Mannaseo bangapseumnida - 만나서 반갑습니다
It's nice to meet you

BTS - The 7Stars To Change My Life

My life was more than hell. Everyone just hated me. I had no hope to continue my life in that way. I tried ending my life twice but there came someone - the 7Stars of my life who changed me, actually changed my life, they changed me. It was like a new life you know like reborn. I got the happiness I had always wished for though my parents in the beginning didn't like me always being into my stars, but they gradually understood why they are my stars. I never had the courage to speak about my feelings or my problems in front of everyone, but now I boldly speak that I want to be happy in my life, I want some space to be me... they taught me to live. Today I thank myself to wait and let them come... and yes BTS wasn't the first group I stanned but none of the other groups gave me the happiness of life... they told me the real meaning of love. Most of my friends have boyfriend's and crushes too and for them obviously their first loves... but for me what my life taught me, what my 7stars taught me, my first love is ME MYSELF. They give me hope, courage, happiness, fashion, and everything I had that I always wished...

Saranghae
army_bts_life

When you need them most

I am a mom, wife, daughter, a former environmental chemist, a nurse and ARMY. In 2014 I started watching Kdramas based on a random google recommendation. I loved the OSTs but just did not get into the Kpop scene or like any certain groups. In 2016 my son and I traveled to Korea for 2 weeks to do a Kdrama tour - Seoul, Jeju, Busan. We ate tteokboki, rode bikes in Hangang Park, went in Namsan tower, all the typical Kdrama touristy things. Fast forward to Hwarang and something about It's Definitely You caught my ear. I added it to my playlist, started listening to more Kpop OST's. In the following year my husband lost his job, we became empty nesters, had a failed business, and moved. Things were not great. One day I caught a BTS MV on YouTube and fell headfirst down the rabbit hole. They were the hope, the joy, the laughter, the fun that I so desperately needed. I spend my time watching all the content I can find,

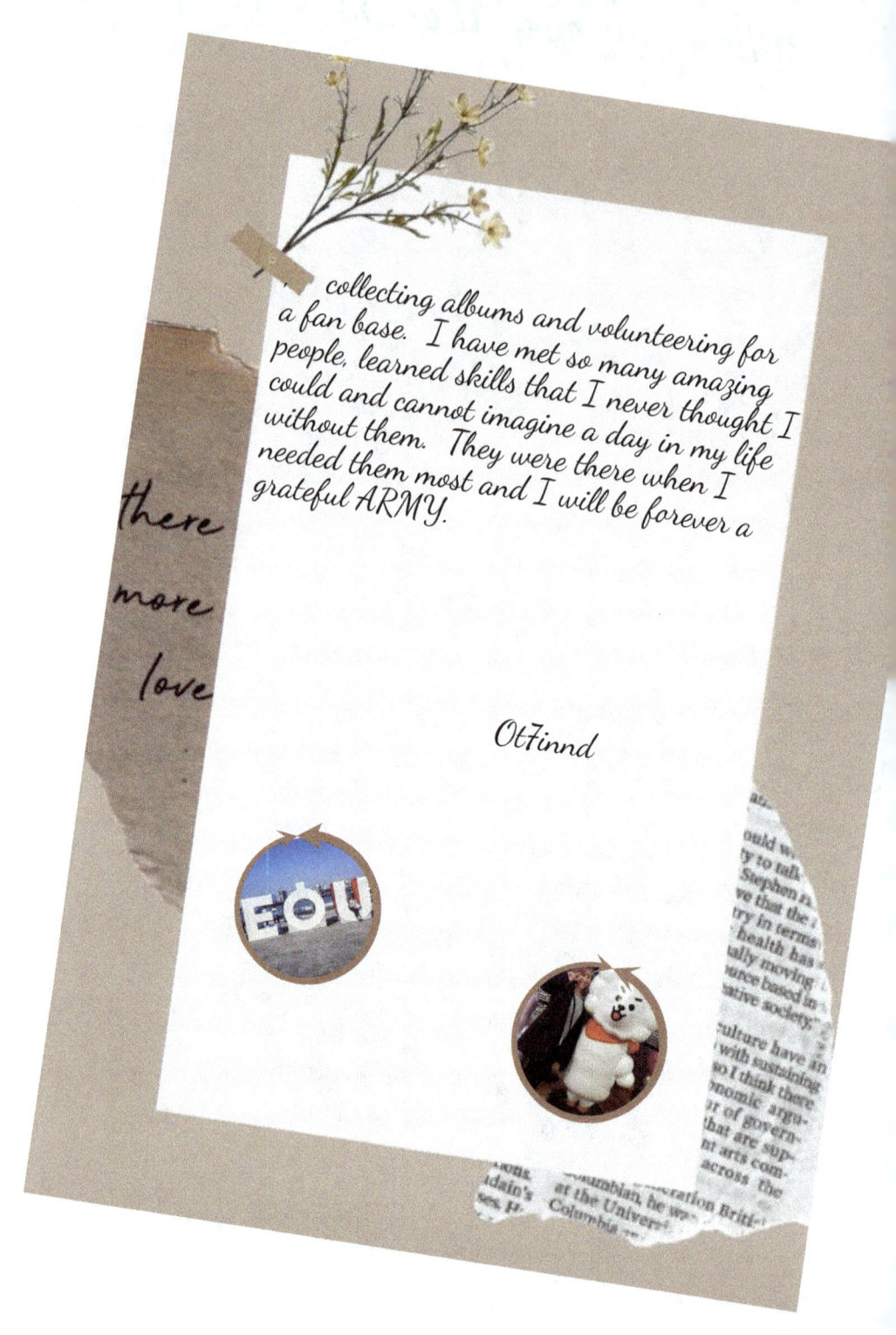

collecting albums and volunteering for a fan base. I have met so many amazing people, learned skills that I never thought I could and cannot imagine a day in my life without them. They were there when I needed them most and I will be forever a grateful ARMY.

Ot7innd

WHAT BTS MEANS TO ME

Back in 2017, my friend who is an army keeps sending me BTS photos and telling me to listen to BTS songs every day, most of my friends also like BTS at that time too, so I decided to search BTS online, watch their videos and listen to their songs. After that, I discovered that they are not only handsome 🤩 but they are also 7 talented boys, composing their own songs and writing their own lyrics 🥺. I watched Fake Love MV and started searching their older videos. Jungkook caught my attention, then I stepped into the world of BTS and started becoming an army. 💜 I decided to become an army because BTS means a lot to me, they are not just an ordinary music group, they worked so hard for all armies around the world, sacrificing their free time, ignoring their health just for all of us. 😭🥰 They are kind and generous, always donating money to help people which inspires me to help those who are in need. They also inspired me so much to become a better person and letting me know the importance of loving ourselves and others. Every single song, words and

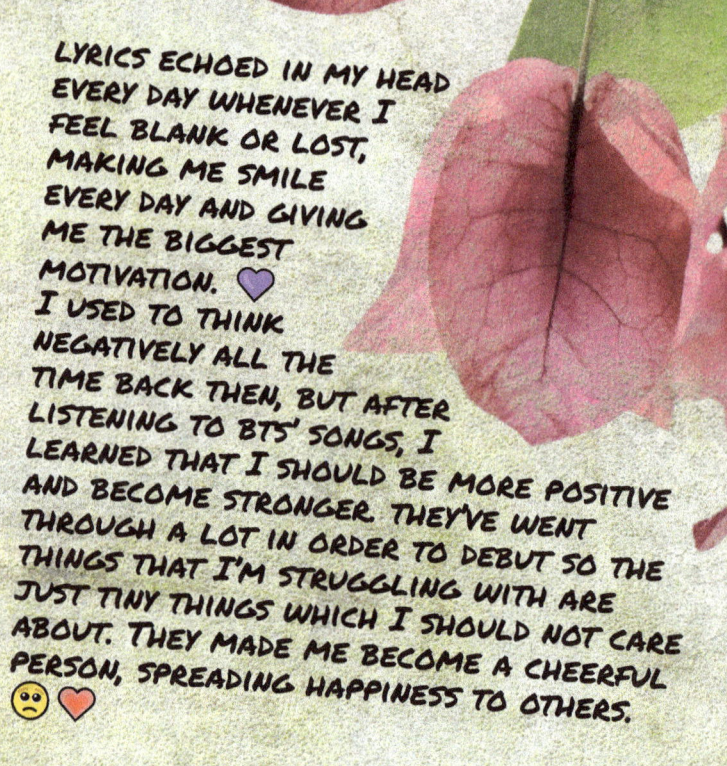

Lyrics echoed in my head every day whenever I feel blank or lost, making me smile every day and giving me the biggest motivation. 💜
I used to think negatively all the time back then, but after listening to BTS' songs, I learned that I should be more positive and become stronger. They've went through a lot in order to debut so the things that I'm struggling with are just tiny things which I should not care about. They made me become a cheerful person, spreading happiness to others. 🥺❤️

TAEWITHKOOKY

'Nothing special, but there's only 1 of me'

My story starts with just an average day channel surfing. I came across BTS performing, I didn't know who they were at that time. It's funny to write this but I honestly can't remember which one caught my eye first, but not because of their Good looks but it was as if "we" had made eye contact. Lol crazy I know. Fast forward and I started off slow into the rabbit hole. Music videos, translations and all that comes with them. I came to understand the message they were speaking. For me it was like getting reacquainted with my best friend. That one who always had good advice when you needed it, always told you "your worth it". Always welcomed you with laughter and a smile. My circle is filled with loved ones. And yet I had a hole inside me that I always covered up, pushed aside and just kept smiling. It was my daily motto. I believe you can usually see one's character just by looking at them. I believe when I channel surfed that day and that instant, that eye contact, the camera, was because it was something I needed. They found me and showed me that hole I had was just doubts and scared of stupid child stuff. I'm a 40+ adult why was I still "not loving myself" when I could love everyone around me easily? Why did I not "speak myself" I listen to everyone around me. That little girl who never felt like her words mattered or was good enough to be good enough, had built a shield with windows. Still present but still scarred. It took a lot of self-searching to admit that. Thanks to Korean translations to songs by this Amazing Group and everyone behind them. I identified with certain lyrics. Slowly I'm becoming a better me. While I'm excepting myself, I talk non-stop about BTS to all those around me. Obviously some are fed up with it, but a couple have asked me questions. I push them on the younger ones because... honestly, EVERYONE needs a best friend who just wants to lift you up. Thank you BTS and their team for being Honest, genuine, and a long-distance friend. You've done more for me then you could ever know. For that reason, I WALK WITH YOU. 💜💜

Laughingirl1

best decision ever

hi there! i'm a 23-year-old mum from poland. i must admit that i was biased (in a bad way) when it came to k-pop because of some girls from my high school. so, when i found out that boy with luv is by a k-pop band, i was really surprised. i'm a halsey fan and that's how i discovered them through their song that was on her spotify playlist. so, when it turned out that it's such a bop, i listened to the whole persona album, and i was so impressed! i had no idea that they rap too, and lyrics just blew me away. i'm ashamed to say it but i didn't expect anything deep from them... i'm glad that i gave them a chance because i never left after. it's been over 2 years now.

bts is like a free therapy session to me. they helped me realize that it's okay to take things slow and to not have a big dream. i'm a student but because of my depression and now being pregnant, i had to take breaks from university, and at first it was hard because all my friends didn't seem to struggle as much as i do but then i thought that it's okay. graduating isn't the most important thing. being healthy for myself and my child is. and i also realized that this is my dream. being the best mum and wife that i can be.

i feel like words can't describe how happy i am to have them in my life. i admire them so much that they talk openly about their own struggles. i think that's why they are so popular; they're relatable, honest, and fun to watch. not mentioning their crazy performance skills... as a person who struggles with mental health, it's so so so important to hear from someone so successful that they have their own problems too. that it's normal and that it's okay to feel bad sometimes. i know they cheer for me and i do the same for them. we don't know each other but i know i can count on them, like we're friends. even though i don't know them, i got to know so many amazing people thanks to them... stanning bts is for sure one of the best decisions i made in my life.

domi

BTS Expanded My Heart

  I wanted to write something deeper, more well thought out but kept stumbling with what I wanted to say so am just going to write from the heart. As relatively new Army, and a much, much older Army, sometimes I feel I have to justify when I discovered BTS, like I am penalized for not having found them earlier. Sometimes, but rarely I believe, people come into your life that make you shine. They make you feel more loving and giving, towards yourself and others. They make you feel joyful and euphoric and good about yourself and your world. That is what BTS did for me. I honestly can't pinpoint when I started discovering BTS and I have tried many times. The best I can do is to say I was aware of them because of their several appearances on various American television shows and award shows for a couple of years. But it wasn't until they appeared on a show in the spring of 2019 that I remember watching them perform Boy with Luv and was just mesmerized by their dancing. Then I will see something from 2018 and remember that I watched it, or even 2017 so I must have been more aware than I realize. Still, I didn't really connect in a deeper way for a while so I don't know how it happened exactly. Most of 2019 was spent with some physical pain and that's where my focus was but all I know is that by New Year's Eve, somewhere along the line I must have been following them more closely because when they appeared on the Rockin' New Year's Eve program, I recall being so proud at how they looked compared to the other performers. Class and style and charm oozed out of them, and I watched them like I had known them for years. Somewhere along the line they had crept into my heart and consciousness without me even being aware of it. From that point forward I had begun the descent into the famous rabbit hole and have never once looked back. Since I didn't know a soul who had even heard of them I had to crawl around the Internet for a few months until I found Weverse and You Tube videos and people on Twitter devoted to BTS so I opened a new account where I felt safe to share my adoration of these seven young men. I even started watching TikTok videos of them. Now every free moment is spent devoted to them. Like everyone says over and over, you find them when you need them most. Or I like to think they found me. Most definitely when I needed them most.

My husband once said to me, "Oh, it's all just entertainment, isn't it?" How little does he know. I have an Asian Studies degree so he said it was only fitting that I would be attracted to them, but I think everyone who becomes Army understands without having to put it into words why we become Army and how we feel about them. It is pretty universal. Being part of a like-minded group, whose sole mission is to make all their dreams come true and support their every happiness fulfills me in a way I never expected to feel. I am filled with happiness and joy and a profound love for these 7 beautiful people that I most likely will never meet and be able to tell them what they mean to me. Yet somehow I feel they know. I am constantly in awe of their talent, their humility, their laughter, their love for each other and their Army, their flawless inner and outer beauty. They have given me more than I could ever thank them for. I could say so much more but this is my story about how they came into my life. I truly, truly love, respect and admire them for the human beings and extraordinary talents that they are. I truly believe there are no finer human beings on this planet than the members of BTS. I am so proud of them and look up to them so much. They have expanded my heart in ways I never dreamed possible.

Susan Finn

You can read more stories on my site!

Discoveringbts.com

Marion

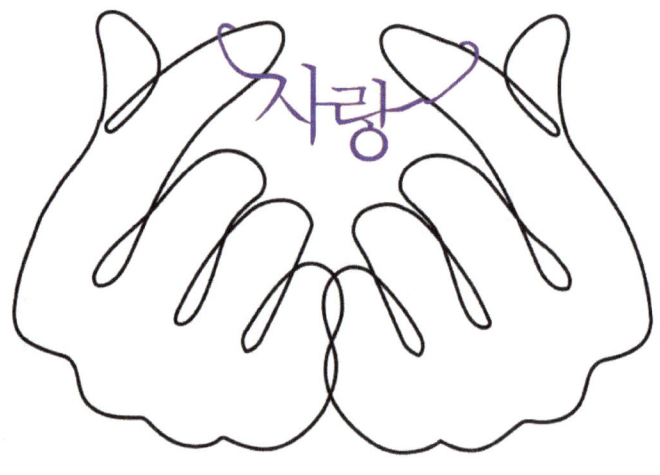

Information

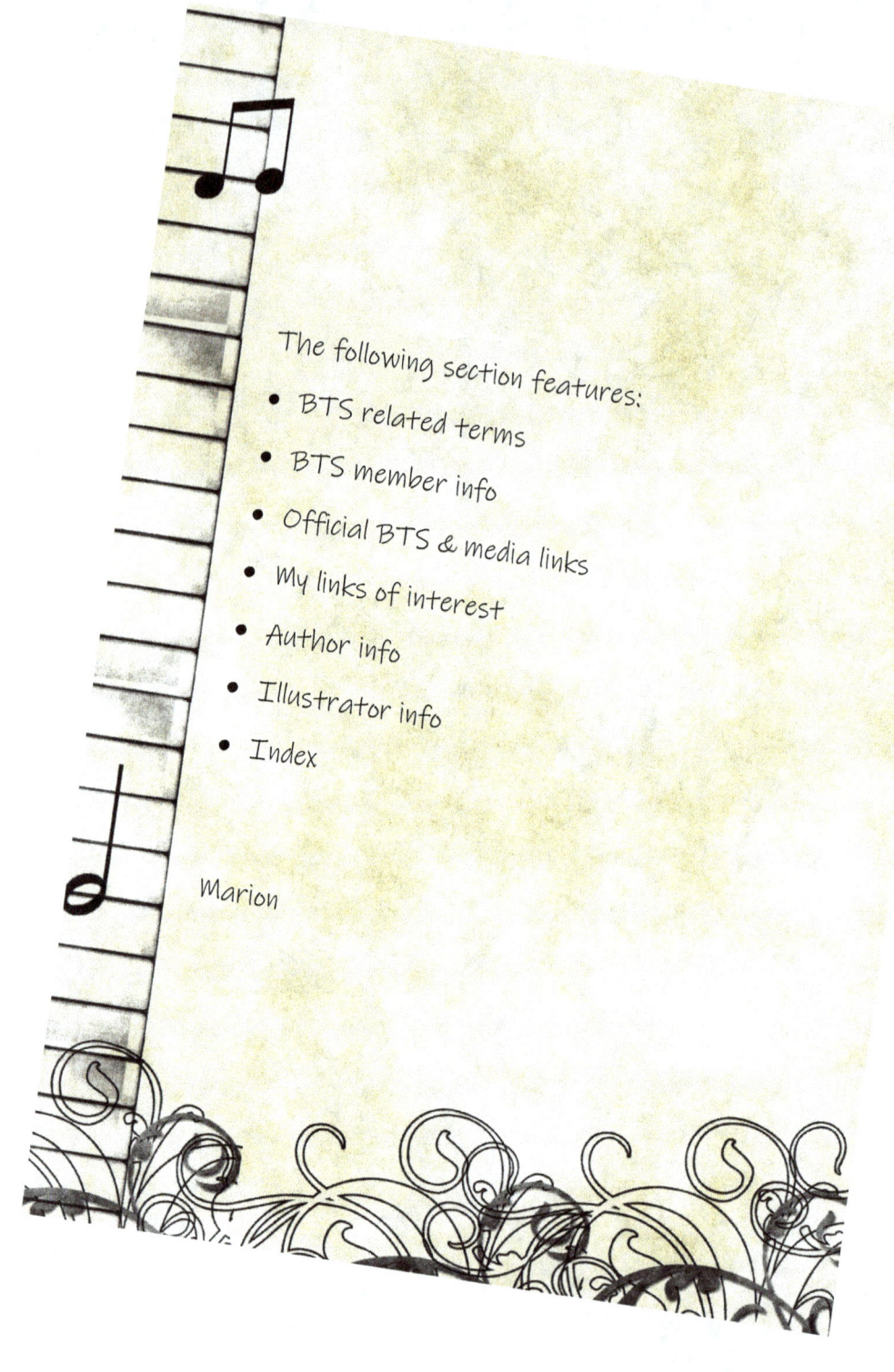

The following section features:
- BTS related terms
- BTS member info
- Official BTS & media links
- My links of interest
- Author info
- Illustrator info
- Index

Marion

BTS Related Terms

By no means a comprehensive list, but it should be a good start.

- **875** - nickname given to BTS by antis (haters of the group).
- **Aegyo** - a Korean word that refers to a "cute" form of speaking or acting that often involves using a higher voice, making cute faces, and using hand gestures.
- **ARMY** - an acronym for "Adorable Representative M.C. for Youth", meaning a fan of BTS.
- **AgustD** - Suga's stage name for his solo rap project.
- **Annyeonghaseyo** - Korean for hello
- **Army bomb** - Every K-pop group also has a custom light-stick. The BTS version is an Army bomb, with a concert mode that connects to Bluetooth, so all the lights twinkle in unison to the beat of the song.
- **Bang PD** - The founder and co-CEO of BigHit Entertainment, BTS' label/management company. His full name is Bang Sihyuk, but fans and guys usually call him Hitman Bang.
- **Bangtan Sonyeondan** - "BTS" (방탄소년단)! or "bulletproof boy scouts". However, on July 4, 2017, BTS officially "re-branded" the acronym to stand for "Beyond The Scene".
- **Bias** - your bias is your favourite member. Many ARMYs also have a "bias-wrecker(s)," or a member(s) they love so much, it makes them question their loyalty to their bias.
- **Bon Voyage** - a nearly annual travel show that began in 2016. They're available to view on VLive. BTS go on day trips, pair up for expeditions, and enjoy a new country.

- **Borahae or "I purple u"** - V (Taehyung) coined this phrase to express his love for ARMY. "Purple is the last color of the rainbow colors," he said. "Purple means I will trust and love you for a long time."

- **BT21** - the BTS collaboration with Line Friends. The members created their own characters, and now there's tons of adorable merch featuring their characters.

- **Comeback** - a sweeping term for putting out new music. While "comeback" often denotes being gone for a long time in Western music, comebacks happen frequently in the world of K-pop.

- **Daesang** - "grand prize." The highest/biggest achievement a K-pop artist can receive for selling the most digital/physical albums. It's awarded at two, end-of-year award ceremonies: the Golden Disk Awards and the Seoul Music Awards.

- **Debut** - a group's first song! BTS debuted in June 2013.

- **Fan cam** - a recording of a K-Pop group's performance focusing on a single member.

- **Fan chant** - chants performed by fans. The most popular is when fans call out the members' names in age order, beginning with the leader of the group - "Kim Namjoon! Kim Seokjin! Min Yoongi! Jung Hoseok! Park Jimin! Kim Taehyung! Jeon Jungkook! BTS!" During Fake Love for instance, fans echo "FAKE LOVE" after the guys sing the words "fake love."

- **FESTA** - the two weeks prior to BTS' anniversary (June 13th), during which the group gifts ARMYs with new photos, behind-the-scenes dance practice videos, unreleased songs, etc.

- **Hangul** - the Korean alphabet

- **Hwaiting** - loosely derived from the English word "fighting." It's a phrase of encouragement like "you got this" or "break a leg." Since the Korean language doesn't have an "F" sound, the English word "fighting" is mispronounced as "hwaiting."

- **Hyung** - an honorific within the Korean language. Koreans use honorifics to refer to people who are older or have a higher status than them. Hyung is used by men to refer to their older male friends/relatives and translates to "older brother."
- **K-POP** - popular music originating in South Korea and encompassing a variety of styles.
- **Line** - a way of grouping the guys. In BTS, there's a rap line (RM, Suga, J-Hope) and a vocal line (Jin, Jimin, V, Jungkook). There's a hyung line (the older guys) and a maknae line (younger guys).
- **Maknae** - a Korean term used to refer to the youngest person in a group. BTS' maknae is Jungkook. He's also often called the "golden maknae," because he's good at almost everything he tries.
- **Merch** - goods associated with BTS. Merch is sold en masse previous to each concert, online at numerous sites, and available at K-POP stores around the world.
- **Mochi** - a Japanese rice cake, but within ARMY, mochi is a popular nickname for Jimin. Fans think his cute, squishy cheeks bear some resemblance to the rice cake.
- **Muster** - muster is a military term that refers to an assembling of troops, and though the ARMY may not be an actual army, BTS still uses the term to refer to a series of special annual concerts.
- **MV** - a music video
- **Namjooning** - exploring and appreciating nature.
- **OT7** - "one true 7" - loving all the members equally.
- **Run BTS** - a variety show that runs weekly featuring the boys playing games, having cook-offs, etc., for points/rewards. Hilarious to watch and usually about 30 minutes in length.
- **Sasaeng** - in South Korean culture, a fan that resorts to stalking, theft, harassment, and other criminal activity to get the attention of a public figure, like an idol or the star of a K-drama.

- **Season's Greetings** - a giant photo shoot done at the start of the new year, often packaged into cute photo cards, calendars and more. Often with an accompanying video.

- **Selca** - a Korean slang word for selfie!

- **Stan** - a verb or a noun, depending on how it's used, meaning to be a fan of something. "I stan BTS!" Note: a "solo stan" is when you ONLY like one member of the group, often dissing the other BTS members.

- **Ship** - short for relationship, and the concept has become something of a staple in fandom culture - if you "ship" two people, it means you love the relationship between them. For instance, "Taekook", meaning Taehyung and Jungkook.

- **Sub-unit** - just a smaller group of members within a larger one. BTS usually splits into sub-units for certain songs.

- **V-LIVE** - while many Western artists mainly use YouTube or Instagram to connect with their fans and post content, idol groups often utilize V Live, a South Korean streaming service.

- **Weverse** - an online community for BTS and ARMYs to connect. Like a "fan cafe". Many other artists use it too. There's also a Weverse store.

Members of BTS

In Korea, family names are first, followed by given names.
Opposite page (L to R): Jungkook, V, Suga, Jin, RM, Jimin, J-Hope
Photo courtesy of Depositphotos.com

Real Name	Stage Name	Nicknames
Kim Nam-joon	RM	Joon, Joonie, Namjoonie
Kim Seok-jin	Jin	Worldwide Handsome, Jinnie, Seokjinnie
Min Yoon-gi	Suga	AgustD, Yoongles, Lil Meow, Min Genius, Yoongs
Jung Ho-seok	J-Hope	Hobi, Seokie
Park Ji-min	Jimin	Mochi, Jiminie
Kim Tae-hyung	V	Tae, TaeTae, Taeyungie
Jeon Jung-kook	Jungkook	Kookie, JK, Golden Maknae, Koo, Jungkookie

Official BTS & Media Links

- Official website: bts.ibighit.com
- Official blog: btsblog.ibighit.com
- Instagram: instagram.com/bts.bighitofficial
- VLive: vlive.tv/channel/FE619
- Twitter: twitter.com/BTS_twt
- Facebook: facebook.com/bangtan.official
- Tiktok: tiktok.com/@bts_official_bighit?
- RUN BTS: vlive.tv/tags/RUNBTS
- BangtanTV - YouTube: youtube.com/channel/UCLkAepWjdyImXSltofFvsYQ
- HYBE Labels - BTS - YouTube: youtube.com/playlist?list=PL_Cqw69_m_yz4JcOfmZb2IDWwIuej1xfN
- Weverse Shop: weverseshop.io/

My Links of Interest

- Discovering BTS: discoveringbts.com

- Proud Daughter Publishing: prouddaughterllc.com

- Marion's Mumblings: waltsdaughter.blogspot.com/

- Twitter: twitter.com/MondayMarionJ

- Our Sponsor, The Comfy Sweatshirt
  Use special code "DiscoverBTS" when ordering.
  etsy.com/shop/TheComfySweatshirt

- The Story of Q - my tween sci-fi series
  storyofq.com

# An Afterword

Throughout the process of writing this book, I've questioned whether I'd be able to convey all my thoughts and feelings about BTS. I'm certain that somewhere along the way I'll have regrets, knowing that things were never penned to these pages. However, I guess it's like that with anything that fills us with passion. How can you ever adequately express what's in your heart?

I've followed many an artist over the years, and it's not very often that I also like them as persons. It's certainly not a requirement, but how refreshing is it when you also genuinely love the individual(s) behind the art? It's so nice to be able to say, I'd love to be friends with anyone of them. And it's even more uplifting that none have become untouchable, smug stars, and that they seem even more approachable now more than ever.

How many of us have added "namjooning" to our vocabularies? Now when I grab my camera and head off to the park, I'm namjooning—enjoying the great outdoors, exploring my world, and capturing all that nature has to offer. I've always been a nature gal, but did Namjoon also motivate you to pay more attention and learn more about your surroundings?

How many of you tried painting for the first time after watching them color huge canvases in episodes of In the Soop? Or maybe you were encouraged after watching them cook during one of their shows. Whatever it was, I hope they inspired you to grow.

Speaking for myself, I know the Covid years would have been much tougher for me, had it not been for seven men from South Korea, because they made every day a little easier to bear.

We've seen them start with nothing other than the clothes on their backs and their lifelong ambitions. They pressed on even when things weren't very promising. How many times were they tempted to throw in the towel, yet they persevered, put in twelve hours workdays, and left the naysayers along the wayside. They overcame adversity and showed us that hard work, tenacity, and determination *do* pay.

So, in conclusion, I can only hope that my story and the stories from numerous contributors have instilled a certain sense of awe and curiosity and inspired you to step outside your comfort zone. And maybe, just maybe, open your heart to BTS.

P.S. As a self-published author, I *solely* rely on reviews and word of mouth, since I don't have an agency to promote my book. So, please take a few minutes of your time and share a review on Amazon, Etsy, or social media. Your assistance is greatly appreciated. It's ARMY looking out for each other.

Index

Information

    BTS Related Terms •234

    Members of BTS •238

    My Links of Interest •241

    Official BTS & Media Links •240

Stories

    'Nothing special, but there's only 1 of me' - Laughingirl1 •222

    A day may come when we lose, but it is NOT TODAY! - WikiNui7 •126

    A Family Affair - Still Paris •152

    A Journey of a lifetime: my story with BTS - Viri •108

    A Not So Special, Special Story - Jooniebot •79

    A Traumatic Time - Empress •172

    Angels of my Life - Leisha •107

    Army With Love - tori_edits •75

    Bangtan Sonyeondan: How 7 artists from Korean helped me discover myself - Shreya_005 •64

    Beautiful. Timely. Special: My Journey with BTS - absolutred16 •212

    Best Decision Ever - domi •224

    Blood, Sweat and What?? - Goldilocks81 •208

    BTS - The 7Stars To Change My Life -

    army_bts_life •217

    BTS are my saviours - MB •186

    BTS Brings Magic Into My Life - Whisper •166

    BTS Expanded My Heart - Susan Finn •226

    BTS Gave Me Back My Smile - Maria_V_tae •148

    BTS is Part of My Life Story - Juujeee7 •90

    BTS My Happiness - Bhuvi Mangia •140

    BTS saved me through the pandemic - JK Fan •202

    BTS Saved Me: A Time of Learning to Love Myself - Sarah •196

    BTS, my parenting tip - Dreamgiver •121

    BTS, the heroes of my life - Sumaia •136

    Delayed Reaction - Kimberly •116

    Depression and a Debt of Gratitude - Whispering2t •68

    Finding Strength in Broken Wings - Jodie DeGruy-Fowler •96

    Growing Up With BTS - Cloudin •112

    Growth: Discovering BTS, &; Myself - @narwhalzipan •160

    Happiness - Garima •102

    Happy Place - Annasanchez2x •156

How BTS Found Me - skorealove_us •159

I "Broke the Silence" - Peach •60

I Just Wanted to Learn Their Names - Gail •88

Kim Tae-hyung Mystery - Dana Shree •143

Losing Everything and Finding Love - Angelize •118

Lost and Found - Ctmdunham •123

Love at the Right Track - Mooniea •111

Magic Shop - kimnuhaaa •95

My ARMY Adventure - Juncel Marcial •182

My Galaxy of Eternal Happiness and Love - Lia Strike •92

My Journey - Dragonmaid49 •125

My Journey to the Purple Land - Emmaculate Baloyi •103

My Life Before BTS - Keerthu •200

My summer vacation (with BTS) - From a high school math teacher... - Guang-Yin Swanland •70

My Untold Story - Pakiza/Arzoo •84

New Life With BTS - tataelephant •178

The Beginning - Jessa2727 •50

The Best Worst Moments in Life - Kedysha •174

The Day Time Stood Still - 5/19/19 - Muneca •46

The Dream - ShookieNuna •80

The Gift of BTS - daydreeem •204

The Morning Will Come Again - Shambhavi •100

The New Discovery - Robbyneils •138

They Saved Me - hhryt •134

To Samsung Ads and Beyong - Maris15 •42

To the boys who played by different rules - tiredladki •76

TO THE PURPLE OCEAN - MeenuMalu •44

We Find Them When We Need Them The Most - Bhavya 101 •74

What BTS Means to ME - TaeWithKooky •220

When you need them most - OtFinnd •218

You're my worst kept secret - Popfrench •144

Youth is Not Over - Athena2020 •180

Yup, Army for Life - BTSmommy305 •52

Zero O'Clock - unsinkableamy •128

김태형 미스터리 - Dana Shree •142

About the Author

Marion lives in a rural town in northern Michigan with her husband Lee. Among her numerous interests are writing/editing/publishing, history, music, cooking, science, perennial gardening, birding, photography, watching football and auto-racing, website, and video design, reading, remodeling/redecorating, jigsaw puzzles, playing scrabble, volunteering in her community, and of course BTS! The word 'boredom' does not exist in her dictionary. She has a great sense of humor and loves to surround herself with like-minded friends and family.

About the Illustrator

Yup, that's me too! The original cover image was photographed by me during the summer of 2021 in Port Austin, MI, overlooking Lake Huron, and transformed into a watercolor for this book.

www.ingramcontent.com/pod-product-compliance
Lightning Source LLC
Chambersburg PA
CBHW071957290426
44109CB00018B/2052